The Valley of Fear

Sir Arthur Conan Doyle

Level 3
(1600-word)

IBC パブリッシング

はじめに

　ラダーシリーズは、「はしご（ladder）」を使って一歩一歩上を目指すように、学習者の実力に合わせ、無理なくステップアップできるよう開発された英文リーダーのシリーズです。

　リーディング力をつけるためには、繰り返したくさん読むこと、いわゆる「多読」がもっとも効果的な学習法であると言われています。多読では、「1. 速く　2. 訳さず英語のまま　3. なるべく辞書を使わず」に読むことが大切です。スピードを計るなど、速く読むよう心がけましょう（たとえば TOEIC® テストの音声スピードはおよそ 1 分間に 150 語です）。そして 1 語ずつ訳すのではなく、英語を英語のまま理解するくせをつけるようにします。こうして読み続けるうちに語感がついてきて、だんだんと英語が理解できるようになるのです。まずは、ラダーシリーズの中からあなたのレベルに合った本を選び、少しずつ英文に慣れ親しんでください。たくさんの本を手にとるうちに、英文書がすらすら読めるようになってくるはずです。

《本シリーズの特徴》

- 中学校レベルから中級者レベルまで5段階に分かれています。自分に合ったレベルからスタートしてください。
- クラシックから現代文学、ノンフィクション、ビジネスと幅広いジャンルを扱っています。あなたの興味に合わせてタイトルを選べます。
- 巻末のワードリストで、いつでもどこでも単語の意味を確認できます。レベル1、2では、文中の全ての単語が、レベル3以上は中学校レベル外の単語が掲載されています。
- カバーにヘッドホーンマークのついているタイトルは、オーディオ・サポートがあります。ウェブから購入／ダウンロードし、リスニング教材としても併用できます。

《使用語彙について》

レベル1：中学校で学習する単語約1000語

レベル2：レベル1の単語＋使用頻度の高い単語約300語

レベル3：レベル1の単語＋使用頻度の高い単語約600語

レベル4：レベル1の単語＋使用頻度の高い単語約1000語

レベル5：語彙制限なし

CONTENTS

Part 1
The Tragedy of Birlstone 1

Part 2
The Scowrers

読みはじめる前に

[**物語の解説**]　*The Valley of Fear*（恐怖の谷）は、シャーロック・ホームズシリーズの最後の長編小説です。2部構成となっており、第1部で事件の概要と解決に至るまでのホームズの推理を、第2部で事件の背景となった「恐怖の谷」と呼ばれるアメリカの炭鉱街・ペンシルベニア州ヴァーミッサ峡谷（Vermissa Valley）での事件を記しています。事件の黒幕には、ホームズの終生のライバル、ジェームズ・モリアーティ教授がいるとされます。

　第2部は第1部の20年前に遡ると書かれていますが、表記には矛盾があり、二つの事件が起きた年代にはさまざまな解釈があります。

[**物語のあらすじ**]　ホームズはポーロック（偽名）という男から届いた、数字とアルファベットが羅列された暗号文の解読に当たっていた。そこに書かれていたのは、バールストン荘に住むダグラスという金持ちに危険が迫っているという内容だった。そこへ時を同じくして訪ねてきた刑事から、暗号通りの殺人事件が発生したと聞かされたホームズは、事件の背後に宿敵モリアーティ教授が絡んでいると疑い捜査に乗り出す。

　顔がめちゃくちゃになった銃殺死体、部屋に置かれていた片方だけの鉄アレイ、堀に囲まれた館からの脱出トリック、過去を語りたがらないダグラスが口にした「恐怖の谷」という言葉——。謎多き館に残された数少ない証拠からホームズが探り出した驚くべき事件の真相とは。

実はこの事件の背景には、20年前、数千マイル離れたアメリカの地で繰り広げられた闘いの果てに、劇的な結末を迎えた恐怖の復讐劇があった。

単語リスト

本書で使われている用語です。わからない語は巻末のワードリストで確認しましょう。

- [ ] almanac
- [ ] boarding-house
- [ ] Bodymaster
- [ ] branded
- [ ] cipher
- [ ] dazed
- [ ] discourse
- [ ] drawbridge
- [ ] faked
- [ ] freeman
- [ ] indecision
- [ ] moated
- [ ] nom-de-plume
- [ ] pantry
- [ ] restful
- [ ] Scowrers
- [ ] sill
- [ ] unfold

主な登場人物

Sherlock Holmes シャーロック・ホームズ　鋭い観察眼と推理力、そして犯罪に関する膨大な知識をあわせ持つ私立探偵。ロンドンのベーカー街221Bに下宿している。

John H. Watson ジョン・H・ワトソン　医師。ホームズのよき相棒でこの物語の語り手。ベーカー街221Bでホームズと同居している。

Professor Moriarty モリアーティ教授　ホームズの宿敵。ロンドンで暗躍する悪党一味を束ねる犯罪者。

Fred Porlock フレッド・ポーロック　モリアーティ教授の部下。ホームズに宛てた手紙で使用しているペンネーム。

Inspector MacDonald マクドナルド警部補　ロンドン警視庁の刑事。事件現場にホームズたちを連れていくためにやってくる。

White Mason ホワイト・メーソン　サセックス州警察の刑事。

Sergeant Wilson ウィルソン巡査部長　バールストン警察の刑事。

John Douglas ジョン・ダグラス　バールストン荘の主人。アメリカの金鉱で成功した資産家。銃殺されて顔が原形をとどめていない状態で発見される。

Mrs. Douglas ダグラス夫人　ジョンより20歳ほど若くて美しい妻。夫の過去のことをよく知らないらしい。

Cecil Barker セシル・バーカー　ダグラス夫妻と親しい資産家。度々バールストン荘に宿泊しており、事件当日も居合わせていた。

Ames エームズ　バールストン荘の老執事。

Mrs. Allen アレン夫人　バールストン荘の家政婦。

Jack McMurdo ジャック・マクマードー　シカゴからヴァーミッサ渓谷にやってきた。のちに秘密結社「自由民団（Order of the Freemen）」の「スカウラーズ（Scowrers）」の団員となる。

Mike Scanlan マイク・スキャンラン　スカウラーズの団員。

Jack McGinty ジャック・マギンティ　スカウラーズの支団長。

Morris モリス　スカウラーズの団員。

Teddy Baldwin テディ・ボールドウィン　スカウラーズの団員。エティーの婚約者。

Ettie Shafter エティー・シャフター　若いドイツ人女性。下宿屋の娘。マクマードーと恋に落ちる。

James Stanger ジェームズ・ステンジャー　地元新聞の編集長。スカウラーズに批判的な記事を掲載する。

Captain Marvin マーヴィン警部　シカゴからヴァーミッサ渓谷にやってきた。

Birdy Edwards バーディ・エドワーズ　ピンカートン探偵局員。随一の腕利きで、スカウラーズの調査に乗り出す。

Steve Wilson スティーヴ・ウィルソン　バーディが調査のために使っている偽名。

PART 1

The Tragedy of Birlstone

Chapter 1
The Warning

Sherlock Holmes and I were in his study. He was leaning his head on his hand and staring at a letter which he had just received, studying it very carefully.

"It's Porlock's writing," he said, thoughtfully. "There's no doubt, though I've seen it only twice before. But if it is Porlock, then it must be of the greatest importance."

"Who then is Porlock?" I asked.

"Porlock, Watson, is a nom-de-plume. Porlock is very important, not for himself, but for the great man with whom he is in touch. You have heard me speak of Professor Moriarty?"

"The famous scientific criminal—?"

"Famous among criminals, yes, but greatly respected as a professor and author by most people who do not know of his other activities."

"But you were speaking of Porlock."

"Ah, yes, Porlock is the only weakness in Moriarty's organization that I have been able to find so far. Encouraged by a little money, he has once or twice given me valuable information in advance. I cannot doubt that, if we had the cipher, we would find that this message has something to do with Moriarty's darker dealings."

I rose, leaned over Holmes and looked at the strange paper, which read:

534 C2 13 127 36 31 4 17 21 41
DOUGLAS 109 293 5 37 BIRLSTONE
26 BIRLSTONE 9 127 171

"What do you think, Holmes?"

"It is clearly a secret code, the numbers representing the pages of some book. Until I am told which book and which page, however, I am powerless. It's likely we will receive some more information soon."

Holmes was right, and within a few minutes Billy the page appeared with the very letter we were expecting.

"The same writing," remarked Holmes, as he opened the letter, "and actually signed," he added, in a happy voice. But, as he read the note his tone became more serious. "Dear me, I trust that the man Porlock will come to no harm."

"Dear Mr. Holmes,

"I can no longer help you. It is too dangerous. He came to me suddenly and almost saw the letter I was writing to you. I cannot send you the cipher. Please burn the previous message, which is now of no use to you.

"FRED PORLOCK"

"Friend Porlock is clearly scared out of his senses."

"Then why did he write at all?" I wondered.

"Because he feared that I would come around asking questions about him."

"Of course," I said. "But it is maddening to think that an important secret lies here undiscovered."

Sherlock Holmes lit his pipe and leaned back, staring at the ceiling, thoughtfully. "I wonder!" he began. "The book Porlock writes of, what do we know about it?"

"Nothing," I said simply.

"Well, well, it's not that bad. The first message begins with a large 534, does it not? We may suppose that this is a page number; so our book must be a long one. The next sign is C2. What do you think of that, Watson?"

"Column!" I cried.

"Wonderful, Watson. So, now we must think of a long book, printed in double columns. One more thing, my dear Watson; if the book had been an unusual one, Porlock would have sent it to me. Therefore, it must be a very common one."

"A Bible!" I cried excitedly.

"Good, Watson, but
not good enough. I can't
imagine a book less
likely to be used by one
of Moriarty's associates.
And besides, there are
so many different vol-
umes of the Bible and
they all have different
page systems."

"An almanac!"

"Excellent, Watson! It is in common use,
has the right number of pages and has double
columns."

He picked up the almanac he always keeps
on his desk.

"Here is page 534, column two. Write down
the words, Watson! Number thirteen is 'there,'
number one hundred and twenty-seven is
'is'—'There is'"—Holmes's eyes were shining
with excitement as he counted the words—
"'danger.' Ha! Wonderful! Put that down,
Watson. 'There is danger—may—come—
very—soon—one.' Then we have the name

'Douglas'—'rich—country—now—at—Birlstone—sure—is—urgent.' There, Watson! The meaning is quite clear. Some evil is intended against one Douglas, a rich country gentleman."

Holmes was still smiling at his success as the door opened and Inspector MacDonald of Scotland Yard entered. He was a physically strong man but clever and quiet-natured. Twice in his work Holmes had helped him to succeed. For this reason the Scotsman showed a deep respect for Holmes.

"Ah, Mr. Mac," he said. "I fear that this means there is some problem."

The inspector was about to answer Holmes when he stopped suddenly, and stared with a look of surprise at the paper on the table.

"Douglas!" he cried. "Birlstone! What's this Mr. Holmes? Where on earth did you get these names?"

"It's a coded message that Watson and I have just solved. But why? What's wrong with the names?"

The inspector looked at us in a strange way. "Just this," he said, "that Mr. Douglas of Birlstone was murdered last night!"

Chapter 2
Sherlock Holmes Discourses

It was one of those moments for which my friend existed.

"Remarkable!" he said. "Remarkable!"

"You don't seem surprised."

"Interested, Mr. Mac, but hardly surprised. I receive word warning that a certain person is in danger, and, within the hour I learn that the person is dead. I am interested, but, as you see, not surprised."

"I was going down to Birlstone this morning. I wanted to see if you would come with me. But from what you say perhaps we might be doing better work in London."

"I rather think not," said Holmes. "Though

the coded message comes from one in Moriarty's circle, we would waste our time trying to find anything about it here."

"Ah, Moriarty," the inspector said. "He's the professor I've heard you talk about?"

"Exactly!"

Inspector MacDonald smiled. "I will not hide from you, Mr. Holmes, that I have looked into the man and have even had a talk with him. He seems very respectable and clever."

Holmes laughed softly. "Tell me, Friend MacDonald, this pleasing meeting was, I suppose, in the professor's study?"

"That's so."

"A fine room, is it not? Did you happen to see a picture over the professor's head?"

"Yes, I saw the picture—a young woman with her head on her hands."

"That painting was by Jean Baptiste Greuze, a famous French artist who lived between 1750 and 1800."

MacDonald smiled weakly. "Your thoughts move a bit too quick for me, Mr. Holmes. What is the connection between this painter and the affair at Birlstone?"

"See if this helps you. In the year 1865, a picture by Greuze was sold for more than forty thousand pounds, and may I remind you that the professor's salary is only seven hundred a year."

"Then how could he buy — "

"Exactly! How could he?"

"That's remarkable," said the inspector thoughtfully.

Holmes smiled, as he always enjoyed being admired. "Yes, the picture shows him to be a very wealthy man. But how did he become so wealthy?"

"You mean he has a large income and must earn it outside the law?"

"Exactly. Of course, I have dozens of reasons for thinking so — "

Before my friend could go on about Moriarty's crimes, Inspector MacDonald brought him back to the matter of Porlock.

"Anyhow, what is really important is that there is some connection between the professor and the crime at Birlstone. You got that from the warning received through the man Porlock. Can we get any further than that, Mr. Holmes?"

"We may look at the reasons for the crime. Firstly, I must tell you that Moriarty has very strict control over his people. He uses only one punishment, death. Perhaps Douglas had in some way angered the chief and he was punished to put the fear of death into the other men.

"Another suggestion is that the death was planned by Moriarty as part of his business." Holmes continued. "Was there anything stolen?"

"I have not heard."

"Well, whatever it may be, we must look for the solution down at Birlstone. While we are on our way, Mr. Mac, I will ask you to tell us all about the case so far."

As we traveled by cab to Birlstone, the inspector

told us of a letter he had received early that morning from White Mason, a local Sussex detective.

"The official report gives the name John Douglas as the murdered man. It mentioned that the man had been shot in the head by a shotgun and that the hour of the alarm was close to midnight last night. It added that the case was clearly one of murder, but no arrest had been made, and that the case was certainly a very strange one. That's all that we have at the moment, Mr. Holmes."

"Then we shall leave it at that, Mr. Mac. I can see only two things at the moment—a great criminal brain in London, and a dead man in Sussex. It's the connection between them that we are going to find."

Chapter 3
The Tragedy of Birlstone

Now, for a moment I will describe the events that took place before we arrived on the scene.

The village of Birlstone is a small and very old group of houses in the north of Sussex. Recently, a number of wealthy families have moved there to enjoy its beauty and natural country charm.

About half a mile from the town, standing in an old park, is the ancient Manor House of Birlstone, parts of which date back to the seventeenth century. A moat forty feet wide, but only a few feet deep, surrounds the house. The ground floor windows are within a foot of the water. The only approach to the house is over a drawbridge, which is pulled up at night—a very important fact to the case.

The house had not been lived in for some years when Mr. John Douglas and his wife moved in. Douglas was a remarkable man, about fifty, with a strong face and a youthful figure. He soon became popular among the villagers, attending their concerts where he sang in a rich voice. He seemed to have a lot of money, gained from the California gold fields. His wife, a beautiful, tall, dark woman, was some twenty years younger than him, but they appeared to have a very happy family life. It was noticed, however, that Mrs. Douglas knew little of her husband's past life in America and seemed quite nervous if her husband was ever late in returning home.

One other person was present at the time of the murder, Cecil Barker of Hampstead. He was a frequent and welcome visitor at the Manor House, an Englishman, who had met Douglas in America. He appeared to be a rather wealthy man, unmarried and somewhat younger than Douglas, forty-five at the most. A tall man, he had a handsome face with sharp black eyes. He was friendly with Douglas and no less friendly with his wife—a friendship that more than once seemed to anger the husband, the servants had noticed.

It was at eleven forty-five on the night of January 6th that the first alarm reached the small local police station. On arriving at the Manor House, Sergeant Wilson, the local policeman, had found the drawbridge down and the whole house in a state of shock. Only Cecil Barker seemed in control of himself and had asked the sergeant in. The village doctor had just arrived and the three men entered the study together.

The dead man lay on his back in the center of the room. He was wearing a pink dressing gown and carpet slippers. One look at the body was enough to show the doctor that he was not needed. The man had

been terribly hurt. Lying across his chest was a strange gun—a shotgun with the barrels cut to a foot in length. It was clear that it had been fired at close range as his head and face were not recognizable.

"Nothing has been touched up to now," said Cecil Barker. "You see it all exactly as I found it."

"When was that?" The sergeant had drawn out his notebook.

"It was just half-past eleven. I was sitting by the fire in my bedroom when I heard the shot. I rushed down quickly."

"Was the door open?"

"Yes. Poor Douglas was lying as you see him. The candle was burning on the table and I lit the lamp some minutes afterwards. Then I heard Mrs. Douglas coming downstairs and I rushed out to stop her from seeing this terrible sight. She went back upstairs with Mrs. Allen, the housekeeper, and then I went back into the room with Ames, the butler, who had just arrived."

"But I have heard that the drawbridge is

kept up all night, so how could the murderer have gotten away?" the sergeant asked.

"Look at this!" Barker drew aside the curtain and held the lamp down to show a mark of blood on the window sill shaped like the bottom of a boot.

"You mean that someone used the window to get to the moat and escape?"

"Exactly!"

"Well, how did he get into the house if the bridge was up? What time was it raised?"

"It was nearly six o'clock," said Ames.

"Well then," said the sergeant, "if anyone came from the outside, they must have gotten in across the bridge before six and been in hiding until Mr. Douglas came into the room after eleven."

The sergeant picked up a card which lay beside the dead man. The letters V.V. and the number 341 were written on it in ink. "What's V.V.? Someone's name, perhaps?" The puzzled policeman walked slowly around the room. "Hello!" he cried excitedly, pulling the curtain to one side. "Someone has been hiding here, sure enough." The sergeant held down the lamp and the marks of muddy boots were able to be seen. "It is likely that his main idea was to rob the house, but Mr. Douglas found him. The thief murdered him and escaped through the window."

The doctor had taken the lamp and was carefully looking at the body. "What's this mark?" he asked. About halfway up the dead man's right arm was an odd brown design, a triangle inside a circle. "The man has been branded at some time. What is the meaning of this?"

"I don't know the meaning of it," said Cecil Barker; "but I have seen the mark on Douglas several times in the last ten years."

"It's a strange thing," said the sergeant. "Everything about this case is strange. Well, what is it now?"

The butler had given a cry of surprise and was pointing at the dead man's hand.

"They've taken his wedding ring!" he exclaimed. "Yes, indeed. Master always wore his plain gold wedding ring on the little finger of his left hand and that ring with the rough nugget above it."

"Are you saying," asked the sergeant, "that the wedding ring was below the other?"

"Always!"

"Then the murderer first took off this ring you call the nugget ring, then the wedding ring, and afterwards put the nugget ring back again."

The country policeman shook his head. "Seems to me that the sooner we get London on this case the better. It won't be long now before White Mason is here to help us. Anyway, I'm not afraid to say that it is a bit too difficult for the likes of me."

Chapter 4
Darkness

At twelve o'clock the chief Sussex detective, White Mason, arrived at the Birlstone police station to welcome us. He was a quiet, comfortable man, who looked more like a small farmer than a criminal officer.

"Your room is at Westville Arms," he said. "This way gentlemen, if you please." And in ten minutes we had all found our rooms and were seated downstairs, listening to the events of the Birlstone mystery which have been described in the last chapter.

"Remarkable!" Holmes said as the story unfolded, "most remarkable!"

"I thought you would say so, Mr. Holmes,"

said White Mason, in great delight. "Sergeant Wilson had all the facts. I checked them and added a few of my own. I examined the gun. It was not more than two feet long—it could easily be carried under a coat. And the letters P-E-N were printed between the barrels."

"Pennsylvania Small Arms Company—a well-known American firm," said Holmes.

"Wonderful!" exclaimed Mason, clearly impressed. "No doubt it is an American shotgun. There is some evidence, then, that this man who entered the house and killed its master was an American."

"May I ask whether you examined the far side of the moat to see if there were any signs of the man having climbed out of the water?"

"Yes, I did, and there were no signs, Mr. Holmes."

"Would you mind if we went down to the house at once? There may be some small points which can help us."

"Not at all, Mr. Holmes. I'm sure we are honored to show you all that we know."

"That's the study window," said Mason, as

we neared the Manor House, "the one to the right of the drawbridge."

We walked across the drawbridge and were met by the butler Ames. The poor old man was white from the shock. The village sergeant, a tall, formal man, was still in the study.

"You can go home, Sergeant Wilson," said Mason. "You've had enough. Now, gentlemen, we must ask ourselves whether the murder was done by someone outside or inside the house. If it were someone from inside, why would they use the strangest and noisiest weapon in the world, a weapon that was never seen in the house before? Besides that, only a minute after the alarm was given the whole household was on the spot. It's not possible that in that time the guilty person had time to make footmarks in the corner, open the window, mark the sill with blood, take the wedding ring off the dead man's finger and the rest of it."

"You put it very clearly," said Holmes, "I agree with you."

"Well then, it must have been done by someone from outside the house. The man got into the house before the bridge was raised and hid behind the curtain. There he remained until Mr. Douglas entered the room. There was a very short interview, as the candle shows."

"The candle shows that how?" I asked.

"The candle was a new one, and has not burned more than half an inch," Mason explained. Then, he continued, "So, Mr. Douglas entered the room, put down the candle and the man appeared from behind the curtain. He was armed with a gun and demanded the wedding ring—why, I do not know—then shot Douglas in this terrible way. He dropped his gun and this strange card—V.V. 341—and made his escape through the window and across the moat at the very moment Cecil Barker was discovering the crime."

"Very interesting, but not very likely."

"Come, Mr. Holmes!" cried MacDonald. "You must give us a lead if you think Mr.

Mason's story isn't likely."

"I need a few more facts before I suggest my own story. Can we have the butler in for the moment? ... Ames, I have observed that there is a small cut on Mr. Douglas's jaw. Did you notice it before?"

"Yes sir, he cut himself while shaving yesterday morning."

"Did you ever know him to cut himself shaving before?"

"Not for a very long time, sir."

"He may have known he was in danger," Holmes said.

"He was a little nervous, sir."

"Ha! The attack may not have been entirely unexpected. We seem to be making a little progress, do we not? Now, what about this card? Can you make anything of the writing—V.V. 341—Ames?"

"No, sir."

"What do you think, Mr. Mac?"

25

"Perhaps it's a secret society of some sort, as with the mark upon the arm."

"That's my idea too," said White Mason.

"Well, we can suppose that an agent from such a society makes his way into the house, waits for Mr. Douglas, kills him, and escapes across the moat, after leaving a card beside the dead man, which will tell other members of the society that the death was in revenge. But why this gun, of all weapons? And why the missing ring?"

While talking, Holmes had gone to the window and was closely looking at the bloodmark on the sill. "It is clearly the mark of a shoe, but it is a rather broad one. Strange, because, as far as I can see, the footmarks behind the curtain seem to be made by a thinner shoe. However, they are not very clear. What's this under the table?"

"Mr. Douglas's dumb-bells," said Ames.

"Dumb-bell—there is only one. Where's the other?"

"I don't know, Mr. Holmes."

"One dumb-bell—" Holmes said seriously, and then there was a knock on the door.

A tall, confident-looking, clean-shaven man looked in at us. I guessed that it was Cecil Barker of whom we had heard.

"Sorry to interrupt your meeting," he said, "but you should hear the latest news."

"Has someone been arrested?"

"No. But they've found his bicycle. It is within a hundred yards of the front door."

We inspected the bicycle, which had been pulled out of some bushes near the house. It was dirty and well used, but there was no clue as to the owner.

"But what made the fellow leave it behind?" the inspector asked. "And how has he gotten away without it? We don't seem to be getting far in the case, Mr. Holmes."

"Don't we?" my friend replied thoughtfully. "I wonder!"

Chapter 5
The People of the Drama

"Now that we've finished with the study, perhaps you would like to hear the evidence of some of the people of the house, gentlemen," said White Mason. "We could use the dining room, Ames. Please come yourself first and tell us what you know."

The butler's story was simple and clear and he seemed truthful. He had started working for Mr. Douglas five years ago, when his master had first come to Birlstone. He never saw any signs of fear in Mr. Douglas, but on the day of the murder, he (Ames) had noticed something different about Mr. Douglas. Ames had not gone to bed, but was in the pantry at the back of the house when he heard the bell ring violently. He heard no shot; there were several passages and doors between the pantry and the study. The housekeeper, Mrs. Allen, had come out of her room when she heard the bell and they had gone to the front of the house together.

As they reached the bottom of the staircase, they had seen Mrs. Douglas, who was quite calm, coming down it. Then Mr. Barker had rushed out and begged her not to go into the study.

"For God's sake! Go back to your room!" he cried, "Poor Jack is dead! You can do nothing."

Mrs. Douglas did not scream or cry, and, after a short time, went with the housekeeper back upstairs to her bedroom. Ames and Mr. Barker had returned to the study. The candle was not lit, but the lamp was burning on the table.

They had looked out of the window, but nothing could be seen or heard.

The evidence of Mrs. Allen seemed to fit in with that of her fellow servant. She had been in her room a little nearer to the front of the house when she had heard the ringing of the bell. She was a little hard of hearing, and perhaps that was why she had not heard the shot. She remembered hearing some sound which she thought was the slamming of a door about half an hour before the bell. As for the other servants, they had all gone to bed at the back of the house and could not have heard anything.

Cecil Barker was the next witness. He had very little to add to what he had told the police. He was sure that the murderer had escaped by the window because of the bloodstain on the window sill. Besides, as the bridge was up, there was no other possible way of leaving the house.

Barker said that Douglas was a quiet man, and there were some parts of his life of which he never spoke. He had gone to America when he was a young man and Barker had first met him in California, where they had become partners in mining. They had done very well, but Douglas had suddenly sold out and left for England. Barker had returned to England and they had renewed their friendship.

Douglas had given Barker the feeling that he was in some danger and he always saw the sudden departure as being connected with this danger. He guessed that some secret society was chasing Douglas and would never stop until it killed him. He thought that the card had something to do with this secret society.

"How long were you with Douglas in California?" asked the inspector.

"Five years, altogether."

"Have you ever heard where his first wife came from?"

"I remember him saying that she was German. She died a year before I met him."

"You don't associate his past with any particular part of America?"

"I have heard him talk of Chicago and he also knew of the coal and iron districts."

"Was there anything unusual about his life in California?"

"He liked best to stay and work in the mountains. He would never go where other men were. That is why I first thought that someone was after him. Within a week of his leaving a dozen men were inquiring after him, a mighty hard-looking crowd."

"These men were Americans — Californians?"

"They were Americans, all right, but not from California."

"That was five years ago and you spent five years with him in California. It seems this business must have been very serious to have continued for ten years. Why didn't he go to the police for protection?"

"Maybe it was some danger that he couldn't be protected against."

"Mr. Barker, did you know Mrs. Douglas before her marriage?"

"No, I did not."

"But you have seen a lot of her since?"

Mr. Barker looked a little angrily at the

inspector. "I have seen a lot of him since. If you imagine there is any connection —"

"I imagine nothing, Mr. Barker. But I must ask, was Mr. Douglas completely happy with your friendship with his wife?"

Barker stood for a moment, his face serious and in deep thought, then he spoke. "Poor Douglas had only one fault, and that was his jealousy. He was such a good friend, and yet, if his wife and I talked together, a kind of wave of jealousy would pass over him, and he would start saying the wildest things in a moment. But I'm sure, gentlemen, that no man ever had a more loving wife — and I can say also no friend could be more true than I!"

"You do know that the dead man's wedding ring has been taken?"

"I have no idea what it means sir, but you must never question the lady's honor."

"There is one small point," remarked Sherlock Holmes. "When you entered the room, there was only one candle lit on the table, was there not?"

"Yes, that was so."

"By its light you saw the terrible thing that had happened, and rang at once for help, which arrived speedily, did it not?"

"Within a minute or so."

"And yet when they arrived they found that the candle was out and the lamp had been lit. That seems very remarkable."

Barker looked uncomfortable and he answered after a pause. "There was very bad light. My first thought was to get a better one. The lamp was on the table, so I lit it and blew out the candle."

Holmes asked no further questions and Barker turned and left the room.

Mrs. Douglas then entered the room. Her face was pale, but her manner was calm.

"Mrs. Douglas," said the inspector. "Perhaps you can tell us something which may help. How long was it after hearing the shot were you stopped on the stairs by Mr. Barker?"

"It may have been a couple of minutes. Then Mrs. Allen took me upstairs. It was all like a bad dream."

"Can you give us any idea of how long your husband had been downstairs before you heard the shot?"

"No, I cannot say. He went from his dressing room and I did not hear him go. He went round the house every night; he was nervous of fire."

"You have known your husband only in England, have you not?"

"Yes, we have been married five years."

"Have you heard him speak of anything which occurred in America which might bring some danger to him?"

Mrs. Douglas thought carefully before she answered. "Yes," she said at last, "I have always felt that there was a danger hanging over him. He refused to discuss it with me, but I knew it by certain words that he let fall and by the way that he looked at unexpected strangers. I was certain that he had some powerful enemies and that he was always on guard against them."

"Might I ask," asked Holmes, "what the words were that you heard?"

"The Valley of Fear," the lady answered. "'I have been in the Valley of Fear. I am not out of it yet.'"

"He never mentioned any names?"

"Yes, once, when he was sick with a fever, he spoke a single name, with anger and a sort of horror. McGinty was the name — Bodymaster McGinty. I asked him when he recovered who Bodymaster McGinty was, but he would tell me nothing."

"There is one other point," said Inspector MacDonald. "You have heard, no doubt, that his wedding ring has been taken. Does that suggest anything to you?"

For a moment, I thought I saw a shadow of a smile on the woman's lips.

"I really cannot tell," she answered. "It's certainly very strange."

"Well, we will not keep you any longer," said the inspector.

Mrs. Douglas rose and swept from the room.

Holmes sat with his head on his hands, in deepest thought. Now he rose and rang the bell. "Ames," he said, when the butler entered, "can you remember what Mr. Barker was wearing on his feet last night when you joined him in the study?"

"Yes, Mr. Holmes. He had a pair of bedroom slippers, and they are still under the chair in the hall. I may say that I noticed that they were stained with blood—so were my own."

"That is natural enough, considering the state of the room. Very good, Ames."

A few minutes later we were in the study. Holmes had brought with him the slippers from the hall.

"Strange!" said Holmes, quietly. "Very strange indeed!" He placed the slipper upon the blood mark on the sill. It was exactly the same size.

"Man," cried the inspector, "Barker has marked the window himself! It's broader than any boot mark. But what's the game Mr. Holmes?"

"Ay, what's the game indeed?" my friend repeated thoughtfully.

Chapter 6
A Dawning Light

The three detectives were busy with the details of the case, so I took a walk in the old-world garden which surrounded the house. As I walked towards a spot hidden by bushes, I heard the sound of voices and a woman's laughter. An instant later I saw Mrs. Douglas and the man Barker before they saw me. Her appearance gave me a shock. Her eyes shone with the joy of living and he had an answering smile on his handsome face. But their faces changed when they saw me and Barker came towards me.

"Excuse me, sir," he said, "but are you Dr. Watson?"

I bowed coldly in reply.

"Dr. Watson," said Mrs. Douglas, "you know Mr. Holmes better than anyone. Supposing that a matter were to be brought secretly to his knowledge. Is it really necessary that he should tell the detectives?"

"Mr. Holmes works alone," I said. "But he would not hide anything which would help them solve the case. I can say no more."

I raised my hat and went on my way.

"I wish to hear none of their secrets," said Holmes, when I reported to him what had happened. "It would be too difficult if it comes to an arrest for murder."

"You think it will come to that?"

"My dear Watson, I don't say that we have solved it—but when we have found the missing dumb-bell—"

"The dumb-bell?"

"Dear me, Watson. What is the use of only one dumb-bell? Of course the case depends on the missing dumb-bell."

He lit his pipe and began to talk about his case, almost as if he were thinking aloud.

"A lie, Watson—the whole story told by Barker is a lie. Mrs. Douglas is lying also. But why are they lying? According to their story, the killer had less than a minute after the murder to take the ring, which was under another, from the dead man's finger, to replace the other ring—a thing he never would have done—and to put that card beside the body. Impossible! No, no, Watson, the murderer was alone with the dead man for some time with the lamp lit. Of that I have no doubt at all. Therefore, the shot must have been fired at some time earlier than we are told.

"At a quarter to eleven the servants had all gone to their rooms, except for Ames, who was in the pantry. I have found that no noise made in the study can be heard in the pantry when all the doors are shut. Mrs. Allen, who is somewhat deaf, mentioned that she did hear something like the sound of a door slamming half an hour before the alarm was given. I have no doubt that was the sound of a gunshot.

"If this is so, we have to find what Barker and Mrs. Douglas, if they are not the actual murderers, could have been doing from the time when the sound of the shot brought them down until half past eleven when they rang the bell to call the servants. What were they doing, and why did they not instantly give the alarm?"

"Do you think that Barker and Mrs. Douglas are guilty of murder?"

"My dear Watson," said Holmes, shaking his pipe at me, "I think that Mrs. Douglas and Barker know the truth about the murder, and are hiding it. I am sure they do. But, let us consider, if they are guilty, why the Valley of Fear, or the Boss McSomebody? Why the cut-off shotgun of all weapons—and an American one at that? How could they be so sure that the sound of it would not bring someone on to them? And again, if a woman and her lover murder a husband, are they going to clearly show their guilt by removing his wedding ring after his death? Does that seem likely?"

"No, it does not. So how do you propose to solve the case?"

"I think an evening alone in that study would help me much. I have arranged it with Ames. You smile, Friend Watson. Well, we shall see. By the way, may I borrow that big umbrella of yours?"

"Certainly—but what a poor weapon! If there is any danger—"

"Nothing serious, my dear Watson."

It was nightfall when Inspector MacDonald and White Mason brought some good news.

"Man, I had my doubts that there was ever an outsider," said MacDonald, "but that's all past now. We've had the bicycle identified, and we have a description of our man. Mr. Douglas had seemed nervous since the day before, when he had been at the nearby town of Tunbridge Wells. So we took the bicycle over with us and showed it at the hotels there. It was identified at once by the manager of the Eagle Commercial as belonging to a man named Hargrave, an American, who had taken a room two days before."

"Was there anything to identify this man?" asked Holmes.

"Very little. A cycle map of the country lay on his bedroom table. He had left the hotel after breakfast yesterday morning on his bicycle, and no more was heard of him."

"But what did he look like?" asked Holmes.

MacDonald looked at his notebook. "The hotel people all agreed that he was a man of about five foot nine in height, fifty or so years, with a grayish mustache, and a curved nose."

"Well, that might almost be a description of

Douglas himself," said Holmes. "Did you get anything else?"

"He was dressed in a heavy gray suit with a short yellow overcoat and a soft cap. So, yesterday morning he set off for this place on his bicycle with the gun hidden in his coat, left his bicycle where it was found and waited for Mr. Douglas to come out. But, when it got dark and Mr. Douglas did not appear, he took his chance and approached the house. He slipped into the first room he saw and hid behind the curtain. He waited until half past eleven when Mr. Douglas came into the room, shot him, then escaped across the moat. He left the bicycle, which would be a clue against him, and made his way to London, or some other safe hiding place. How is that, Mr. Holmes?"

"Well Mr. Mac, my end of the story is that the crime occurred half an hour earlier than reported; that Mrs. Douglas and Barker are both hiding something; that they helped the murderer escape—or they reached the room before he escaped—and that they lied about his escape through the window, and they probably let him go themselves by lowering the drawbridge."

"But the lady has never been in America in all her life," said White Mason. "What possible connection could she have with an American murderer which would cause her to help him?"

"Yes, there are some difficulties," said Holmes. "I will make a little investigation of my own tonight, and we shall see what happens."

"Can we help you, Mr. Holmes?"

"No, no!" said Holmes mysteriously. "Darkness and Watson's umbrella are all that I will need."

Chapter 7
The Solution

The next morning after breakfast we found Inspector MacDonald and White Mason at the local police station.

Holmes started the conversation with some surprising words. "Mr. Mac and Mr. Mason, I wish to give you a very serious piece of advice in only four words — stop working the case!"

"What!" cried the inspector. "But the bicyclist, he must be somewhere."

"Yes, yes, and no doubt we shall get him, but don't trouble to trace the mysterious gentleman with the bicycle. I assure you that it won't help you."

"You are holding something back. It's hardly fair of you, Mr. Holmes."

"You know how my methods work, Mr. Mac. But I will hold back for the shortest time possible. I only wish to make my details clear."

"What has happened since last night to give you a completely new idea of the case?"

"Well, I spent some hours last night at the Manor House."

"What were you doing?"

"Ha! I was looking for the missing dumb-bell and I ended up finding it. I can say no more. But gentlemen, meet me here this evening without fail—without fail! And now, I would like you to write a note to Mr. Barker."

Holmes said the following words and Mac-Donald wrote them down, though he didn't look pleased about it.

"DEAR SIR:

"We must drain the moat, in the hope that we may find something which may help our investigation. The workmen will begin early tomorrow morning, so I thought it best to let you know beforehand.

"Now sign that, and send it by hand at about five o'clock. At that hour we shall meet again in this room," instructed Holmes.

That evening Holmes was very serious in his manner, myself very curious and the detectives clearly untrusting and a little angry.

"Well, gentlemen, it is a chill evening; so you'd better wear your warmest coats. Let us get started at once."

We passed along the border of the Manor House park, until we reached some bushes almost opposite the drawbridge. Holmes bent down behind the bushes, and we all followed his example. There was a single light over the gateway and a light in the study. Everything else was dark and still.

"How long is this to last?" asked the inspector finally. "And what is it that we are watching for?"

"That's what we're watching for!" whispered Holmes.

As he spoke we could see someone passing

in front of the light in the study. Suddenly, the window was thrown open and we could see the dark outline of a man's head and shoulders, looking out into the night. Then he leaned forward and seemed to be stirring up the moat with something  which he held in his hand. Then suddenly he pulled something up—a large, round object which he dragged through the window.

"Now!" cried Holmes. "Now!"

We were all upon our feet, running across the bridge and into the room which had been occupied by the man whom we had been watching.

The oil lamp, the glow we had seen from outside, was now in the hand of Cecil Barker, who held it towards us as we entered.

"What is the meaning of all this?" he cried.

Holmes glanced around and then pointed to a wet bundle which lay under the writing table.

"This is what we want, Mr. Barker—this bundle, weighted with a dumb-bell, which you have just raised from the bottom of the moat."

Barker stared at Holmes with surprise in his face. "How did you know anything about it?" he asked.

"Simply that I put it there—or perhaps I should say 'replaced' it there. You will remember, Inspector MacDonald, that I was somewhat curious about the absence of the dumb-bell. So, last night, with the help of Ames, and the crook of Watson's umbrella, I went 'fishing' and came up with this bundle."

Sherlock Holmes put the wet bundle on the table and undid the cord around it. From within he took out a dumb-bell and a pair of boots.

"American, as you see," he remarked, pointing at the toes. Then he laid a long knife on the table and finally he undid a bundle of clothing: underclothes, socks, a gray suit and a short yellow overcoat. He held the overcoat towards the light. "'Neal Outfitter, Vermissa, U.S.A.' I have found that Vermissa is a little town in

51

one of the best known coal and iron valleys in the United States. I remember, Mr. Barker, that you associated the coal districts with Mr. Douglas's first wife. It would surely mean that the V.V. on the card by the dead body might stand for Vermissa Valley, which may be that Valley of Fear of which we have heard. And now Mr. Barker, your explanation."

Cecil Barker's face showed anger, surprise and indecision.

"Well, all I can say is that if there's any secret here it's not my secret, and I'm not the man to give it away," said Barker firmly.

A long silence was then broken by a woman's voice. Mrs. Douglas had been listening at the half opened door, and now she entered the room.

"You have done enough for now, Cecil," she said.

"Madam," said Holmes. "I would strongly urge you to tell the police everything. It may be that I am at fault for not following the hint that you gave to my friend Dr. Watson, but at that time I had every reason to believe that you were directly concerned with the crime. Now I am sure that this is not so. I strongly recommend that you ask Mr. Douglas to tell us his own story."

Mrs. Douglas gave a cry of surprise at Holmes's words. The detectives and I must have cried out, too, as we saw a man come toward us now from a dark corner of the room. Mrs. Douglas turned, and in an instant her arms were round him.

"It's best this way, Jack," she said.

"Indeed, yes, Mr. Douglas," said Sherlock Holmes, "I am sure that you will find it best."

The man stood with the dazed look of one who comes from the dark into the light. It was a remarkable face, clear gray eyes, a strong, short mustache, a square chin and a humorous mouth. He took a good look at us all, and then to my surprise he handed me a bundle of papers.

"I've heard of you," he said in a voice which was not quite English and not quite American. "Well, Dr. Watson, I've been in there two days, and I've spent the daylight hours putting the thing into words. There's the story of the Valley of Fear."

Inspector MacDonald had been staring at the newcomer with the greatest surprise. "Well," he cried at last. "If you are Mr. John Douglas of Birlstone Manor, then whose death have we been investigating for these last two days, and where have you come from now? You seemed to spring out of the floor."

"Ah, Mr. Mac," said Holmes, "when I found the suit of clothes in the moat, it at once became clear to me that the body we had found must have been that of the bicyclist from Tunbridge Wells. Therefore I decided that, with the help of his wife and friend, Mr. Douglas was probably hidden in the house and was awaiting quieter times when he could make his final escape."

"Well, you are about right," said Douglas. "It all came down to this: there are some men that hate me and so long as I am alive and they are alive, there is no safety in this world for me. They chased me out of America, but when I married and settled down in this quiet spot I thought my last years were going to be peaceful. I never explained to my wife how things were. She told you all that she knew, and so did Mr. Barker here; for on the night when this thing happened there was little time for explanations. She knows everything now, however. Gentlemen, the day before these happenings I was over at Tunbridge Wells, and I saw a man in the street. He was the worst enemy I had among them all. I was on my guard all that next day and never went out into the park. After the bridge was up my mind was more restful. But later when I checked the house in my dressing gown, as was my habit, I entered the study with just one candle in my hand and he sprang at me. I saw a knife so I hit him and the knife fell to the floor. A moment later he'd got his gun from under his coat, but I got hold of it before he could fire. We fought for a minute and then the gun fired at his head. I'm afraid his own mother would not have known the face of my sworn enemy, Ted Baldwin.

"Then Barker came hurrying down. I heard my wife coming, and I ran to the door and stopped her. Barker and I waited for the servants to come along. But when there was no sign of them, we understood that they had heard nothing, and it was at that instant that an idea came to me. Baldwin's sleeve had slipped up and I saw the branded mark of the lodge upon his arm. See here!" Douglas turned up his own coat and shirt sleeve to show a brown triangle within a circle exactly like that which we had seen on the dead man. "Then there was his height and hair and figure, about the same as my own, and no one could recognize his face. I put on this suit and Barker and I put my dressing gown on him and he lay as you found him. We tied all his things into a bundle and I weighted them down with the dumb-bell and threw them out the window. The card he had meant to lay upon my body was lying beside his own. I put my other rings on his finger, but I could not remove my wedding ring. I also put a piece of plaster on him where I am wearing one myself.

"Well, that was the situation. I thought if I could hide for a while and then get away where I could be joined by my wife, we should have a chance of living in peace. If they saw in the papers that Baldwin had killed me, there would be an end to all my troubles. I went into this hiding place and Barker did the rest. He opened the window and made the mark on the sill to give an idea of how the murderer escaped. Then he rang the bell and what happened afterward you know."

There was a silence which was broken by Sherlock Holmes.

"Mr. Douglas, how did this man know that you lived here, or how to get into your house?"

"I know nothing of this."

Holmes's face was very white and serious.

"The story is not over yet, I fear," he said. "You may find worse dangers than your enemies from America. I see trouble before you, Mr. Douglas. You'll take my advice and still be on your guard."

And now, my readers, I will ask you to journey back some twenty years in time, and westward some thousands of miles, to America, so that I may tell you a terrible story—so terrible that you may find it hard to believe. And when you have read it, we shall meet once more in those rooms on Baker Street, where our current story will find its end.

PART 2

The Scowrers

Chapter 1
The Man

IT was the fourth of February, 1875. The snow was deep but the railroad was open, and the evening train, which connected all the coal-mining towns, was slowly moving across the plain to Vermissa, a small town in a lonely corner of the country.

In the leading passenger car, a young man sat by himself. He was middle-sized, in about his thirtieth year, and had come all the way from Ireland. He had large, humorous gray eyes and it was easy to see that he wanted to be friendly to everyone.

The young traveler looked out at the dark countryside and sometimes took from his pocket a letter which he studied carefully. Once from the back of his belt, he pulled a gun which was fully loaded. He quickly put it back, but not before it had been seen by a miner who was seated nearby.

"Hullo," said the miner. "You a stranger in these parts?"

"Yes, I heard there was always work for a willing man."

"You may find you need that gun here," said the miner. "Have you any friends?"

"I am one of the Order of Freemen and where there is a lodge I will find my friends."

The miner came closer to the young traveler, sat down, and held out his hand. "I'm Brother Scanlan, Lodge 341, Vermissa Valley. Glad to see you in these parts."

"Thank you. I'm Brother Jack McMurdo, Lodge 29, Chicago."

"Where are you going now?"

"Vermissa."

"Well, I must get off now. But, there's one piece of advice I'll give you: if you're in trouble in Vermissa, go to the Union House and see Boss McGinty. He is the Bodymaster of Vermissa Lodge and he controls everything around these parts. Bye for now." With that, Scanlan left the train.

Two policemen looked at McMurdo from across the train car. "I guess you are new to this part, young man," said one of them.

"Well, what if I am?" McMurdo answered in a rude voice.

"I advise you to be careful in choosing your friends. I don't think I'd begin with Mike Scanlan if I were you."

"What the hell is it to you who are my friends!" yelled McMurdo, so that every head in the car turned to look and the policemen were rather surprised. "I'm not afraid of you! My name's Jack McMurdo—see? If you want me, you'll find me at Jacob Shafter's on Sheridan Street, Vermissa. That's so you know I'm not hiding from you!"

A few minutes later the train stopped at Vermissa and McMurdo got off. As he started walking, one of the miners from the train came up to him.

"Well, you certainly know how to talk to the cops," the miner said with respect. "Let me show you the road. I'm passing Shafter's on my way." So the two men walked through the dirty, ugly town.

"That's the Union House," said the guide, pointing to a hotel. "Jack McGinty is the boss there."

"What sort of a man is he?" McMurdo asked.

"What! You never heard of him or the Scowrers?"

"A group of murderers, are they not?"

"Quiet!" cried the miner. "Man, you won't live long in these parts if you speak in the open

streets like that." The man looked nervously around him as he spoke. "There's the house you want."

"I thank you," said McMurdo, walking up the path and knocking on the door.

It was opened by a young German woman, fair-haired, with a pair of beautiful dark eyes. McMurdo had never seen such a beautiful woman and he stood staring at her without saying a word. At last he said, "Your house was recommended to me by a friend for board."

"Come right in, sir," said the woman. "I'm Miss Ettie Shafter, Mr. Shafter's daughter and I run the house—ah, here comes father."

A heavy, old man came up the path. In a few moments McMurdo explained his business. And so it was that McMurdo came to stay in the Shafter's house, the first step in a long train of events, ending in a far distant land.

Chapter 2

The Bodymaster

McMurdo was a man who made his mark quickly. Within a week he had become the most important person at Shafter's. The young Irishman's joke was always the quickest, his conversation the brightest, his song the best and he drew good humor from all around him. But he showed again and again a sudden strong anger, which made those who met him feel fear and respect.

From the first it was clear that Ettie had won his heart. On the second day he told her that he loved her, and when she talked about someone else, he would not listen.

"You can keep saying no, Ettie," he would

cry, "but the day will come when you say yes, and I am young enough to wait."

McMurdo had gotten a job as a bookkeeper, for he was a well-educated man. This kept him out most of the day and he had not found time to visit the head of the lodge of the Order of Freemen.

One evening, his good German host asked the young man into his private room and started to talk about Ettie.

"It seems to me that you are in love with my Ettie," said Mr. Shafter.

"Yes, that is so," the young man answered.

"Well, I want to tell you right now that it is no use. Someone has already decided to marry her. It is Teddy Baldwin."

"And who the devil is he?"

"He is a boss of Scowrers."

"Who are these Scowrers that you are all afraid of?"

The boarding-house keeper looked frightened and spoke quietly, as everyone did who talked of that terrible society. "The Scowrers," he said, "are the Order of the Freemen!"

The young man stared. "Why, I am a member of that order myself."

"You? I would never have had you in my house if I had known that."

"What's wrong with the order? It is for charity and good."

"Maybe in some places, but not here!"

McMurdo laughed. "That can't be true."

"If you live here long you will see. You will soon be as bad as the rest. It is bad enough that one of these people wants to marry my Ettie, and that I am too afraid to say no, but that I should have another for my boarder? You must leave this very night!"

McMurdo was shocked that he was to be pushed out of the house and away from the girl he loved. He looked for Ettie later that evening and poured his troubles out to her.

"Ettie, I have known you only a week, but you are the very breath of life to me, and I cannot live without you!"

"Oh, Mr. McMurdo," said the young woman. "I have told you that you are too late!" She put her face into her hands. "I wish to heaven that you had been first!"

He put his arms around her as she cried.

"Could you take me away?" she said through tears. "If you would escape with me, Jack, we could take father and live far from the power of these wicked men."

There was a struggle on McMurdo's face. "No, I can't leave here. No harm will come to you, Ettie. As for the wicked men, you may find that I am as bad as the worst of them before we are through. But, hullo, who's this?" A tall, mean-looking man had walked into the room.

Ettie jumped to her feet with alarm. "I'm glad to see you Mr. Baldwin," she said. "This is a friend of mine, Mr. McMurdo."

"Well, mister, this young lady is mine, and you'll find it a very fine evening for a walk."

"Thank you, but I do not feel like taking a walk," answered McMurdo.

"Don't you?" The man's eyes were filled with anger. "Maybe you feel like having a fight then!"

"That I do!" cried McMurdo, jumping to his feet.

"For God's sake, Jack!" cried poor Ettie. "Jack, he will hurt you!"

"I'll choose my own time, mister," Baldwin said as he went out the door.

For a few moments McMurdo and the young woman stood in silence. Then she threw her arms around him.

"Oh, Jack, how brave you were! But it's no use, you must go! Tonight—Jack—tonight! He will kill you. What chance do you have against a dozen of them, with Boss McGinty and all the power of the lodge behind them?"

McMurdo kissed her. "Don't fear for me. I'm a freeman myself. Maybe I am no better than the others. Perhaps you hate me now, too."

"No, Jack, I could never do that! I've heard that there is no harm in being a freeman anywhere but here. But if you are a freeman, Jack, you should go down and make a friend of Boss McGinty."

"I was thinking the same thing," said McMurdo. "I'll go right now."

The bar of McGinty's saloon was crowded as usual, for it was the favorite place of all the rougher men of the town.

McMurdo pushed open the swinging door and went in. At the far end of the bar, stood the famous McGinty himself. He was a black-haired giant and his eyes were a strange dead black color, which gave him a particularly frightening appearance. McMurdo pushed his way through the crowd.

"I'm new here, Mr. McGinty," he said boldly.

"And who told you to see me?"

"Brother Scanlan of Lodge 341, Vermissa. I

recently left Chicago, where I was a member of Lodge 29. I drink your health, sir."

"We don't take folk on trust in these parts, nor do we believe all we're told neither. Come in here for a moment, behind the bar."

McGinty led him to a small room, closed the door, and sat down. For a couple of minutes there was complete silence. Suddenly he bent down and pulled out a terrible looking gun.

"This is a strange welcome," said McMurdo.

"What are you doing here?"

"Working, the same as you—but a poorer job."

"Why did you leave Chicago?"

McMurdo took a worn newspaper cutting from an inner pocket. McGinty glanced at the story of the shooting of one Jonas Pinto, in the Lake Saloon, Market Street, Chicago.

"Why did you shoot him?"

"I was making fake money. This man Pinto was helping me. Then he said he wanted to quit, so I killed him and came out here."

"Why here?"

"'Cause I read in the paper that people weren't too particular in these parts."

McGinty laughed. "Well, you'll be a very useful brother, I'm thinking. We can use a bad man or two among us, Friend McMurdo."

Suddenly Ted Baldwin burst into the room.

"So," he said with an angry look at McMurdo, "you got here first, did you? I must tell you, Boss, about this man."

"We have a new brother here, Baldwin, and it is not for us to greet him in such a way," said McGinty. "Shake hands, man."

"Never!" cried Baldwin.

"What is it then?"

"A young lady. She is free to choose for herself," McMurdo said calmly.

"Is she?" cried Baldwin.

"I should say that she is," said the Boss with a dark stare.

"You are not Bodymaster for life, Jack McGinty, and by God! When it next comes time to vote—"

The Boss sprang at Baldwin like a tiger and closed his hands around the other's neck.

"Easy, Bodymaster!" cried McMurdo, as he dragged him back.

McGinty let go, and Baldwin, shaken and feeling his throat, said, "I have nothing against you, sir."

"Well, then," cried the Boss, "we are all good friends again and that's the end of the matter. The lodge rules with a heavy hand in these parts, Brother McMurdo, if you ask for trouble."

"I surely won't do that," said McMurdo. He held out his hand to Baldwin. "I'm quick to quarrel and quick to forgive."

Baldwin had to take his hand, for the strict eye of the terrible Boss was watching. But his face showed his true feelings.

"You'll have to join Lodge 341, Brother McMurdo. We have our own ways and methods, different from Chicago. Saturday night is our meeting and I expect to see you there," said McGinty.

Chapter 3
Lodge 341, Vermissa

On the following day, McMurdo moved to a boarding-house on the other side of the town. Scanlan, the first man he had met on the train, moved to Vermissa and the two stayed together. Shafter let McMurdo come to meals when he liked, so he still saw Ettie and they grew closer as the weeks went by.

On a Saturday night McMurdo was introduced to the lodge. The group met in a large room at the Union House. Some sixty members met at Vermissa, but altogether there were nearly five hundred members across the whole coal district.

They were mostly older men, with lawless

souls, in truth a very dangerous group of murderers who took a terrible pride in their activities. At first they had tried to keep their actions secret, but no one would dare to speak against them and the law could not stop them.

Three of the men removed McMurdo's coat and rolled up the sleeve of his right arm. Then they placed a thick, black cap right over his head and the upper part of his face, so that he could see nothing.

"Jack McMurdo," said the voice of McGinty, "is your lodge number 29, Chicago?"

"Yes, it is."

"Are you ready to be tested?"

"Yes, I am."

Then he almost screamed out, for a terrible pain shot through his right arm. He bit his lip and tightened his hands to hide the pain.

Then there was loud cheering, the cover was taken from his head. An odd mark burned red and painful on his arm, but he stood smiling among the brothers.

"One last word, Brother McMurdo," said McGinty. "You have already promised secrecy to the lodge. Do you know that the punishment for disobeying me is instant death?"

"I do," said McMurdo.

"Then I welcome you to Lodge 341. Let us drink to our new brother!"

When the drinks had all been finished, the business of the lodge proceeded.

"The first business," said McGinty, "is to send a message to our local newspaper editor, James Stanger." McGinty took a small piece of newspaper from his jacket pocket and began to read.

"LAW AND ORDER!

"TERROR IN THE COAL AND IRON DISTRICT

"Twelve years have now passed since the first killing which proved there is a criminal group among us. From that day these murders have never ceased. These lawless men are known to us. The group is public. How long are we to endure it? Are we to forever live—

"Sure I've read enough of it!" cried the Boss, throwing the paper down.

"Kill him!" cried a dozen voices.

"I protest against that," said Brother Morris, a kind-looking man. "Our hand is too heavy in the valley. James Stanger is an old man and if he is struck down, that will surely bring our end."

"See here, Brother Morris, you should be more careful what you say," said the Bodymaster threateningly.

Morris turned a deadly pale. "I am sorry Eminent Bodymaster and I promise you that I will not question you again."

The Bodymaster relaxed as he listened to the humble words, "Very good, Brother Morris. I would be sad if I had to give you a lesson. And now, boys," he continued, looking round at the company, "It's true that if Stanger were killed, there would be more trouble than we need. But I guess you can give him a hard warning. Can you fix it, Brother Baldwin?"

"Sure!" said the young man, eagerly.

"How many men will you take?"

"Half a dozen, and two to guard the door."

"I think our new brother should go," said the Boss.

Ted Baldwin looked at McMurdo with eyes that showed he had not forgotten nor forgiven. "Well, he can come if he wants," he said in a rude voice.

Later that night, the men gathered in front of a high building. The words "Vermissa Herald" were printed in gold lettering between the brightly lit windows.

"Here," Baldwin said to McMurdo, "you can stand at the door and watch the street."

The other men pushed open the door of the newspaper office and went upstairs. McMurdo stayed below. From the room above came a shout, a cry for help, and then the sound of running feet and falling chairs. An instant later a gray-haired man rushed to the top of the stairs.

He was caught and half a dozen sticks struck him over and over. Baldwin kept hitting the man even after the others stopped. McMurdo rushed up the stairs and pushed him back.

"You'll kill the man," McMurdo said.

"Curse you!" answered Baldwin.

McMurdo pulled his gun from his pocket. "Didn't the Bodymaster order that he was not to be killed?"

"You'd best hurry," cried the man below. "The windows are all lighting up and you'll have half the town here in five minutes."

Leaving the motionless body of the editor at the top of the stairs, the criminals rushed down the street. At the Union House, some of them mixed with the crowd in McGinty's saloon, whispering across the bar to the Boss that the job had been well done. Others, among them McMurdo, went by the side streets to their own homes.

Chapter 4
The Valley of Fear

When McMurdo awoke the next morning his head hurt with the effect of the drink and his arm was hot and sore. Because of the fake money he made, he did not regularly attend his work, so he had a late breakfast, and read the *Vermissa Herald*. It said:

SHOCK AT THE HERALD OFFICE
—EDITOR SERIOUSLY WOUNDED.

... The matter is now in the hands of the police; but it can hardly be hoped that there will be better results than in the past. Some of the men were recognized, so perhaps an arrest will be made. The police are even now searching for the attackers.

McMurdo was thinking about the previous evening and the editor's scared face when he received a message. It read:

I wish to speak to you, but would rather not in your house. You will find me up on Miller Hill. If you come there now, I have something which is important for you to hear and for me to say.

He was not sure who sent it but decided to go. As he walked up the winding path to the top of the hill, he saw a man with a hat low over his face. The man looked up and McMurdo saw Brother Morris, the freeman who had made the Bodymaster angry the night before.

"I wanted to have a word with you, Mr. McMurdo," said the older man, with fear in his voice. "It seemed to me last night that you are new to the ways here and perhaps not as hard as the other men. Can I trust you?"

"Of course!"

"When you joined the Freeman's society in Chicago, did you ever imagine it would lead to crime?"

"If you call it crime."

"Of course it is crime!" cried Morris. "When I came here I was forced to join the lodge and now I can't get away; if I leave the society it means death for me. Oh, it is awful—awful!"

McMurdo smiled. "I think you are a weak man and make too much of the matter."

"Too much! Wait till you have lived here longer. Look down the valley! It is the Valley of Fear, the Valley of Death."

"Well, I'll let you know what I think when I have seen more," said McMurdo carelessly. "What you have said is safe with me. Now I'll be getting home."

"One word before you go," said Morris. "We may have been seen together. They may want to know what we have spoken about. Let us say that I offered you a job at my store."

"And I refused it. Well, goodbye, Brother Morris, and good luck for the future."

That same afternoon, as McMurdo sat smoking, the door swung open and the door frame was filled with the huge figure of Boss McGinty.

"What were you speaking to Brother Morris about on Miller Hill this morning?"

The question came so suddenly that McMurdo was glad to have his answer prepared. He laughed. "Brother Morris did not know about the fake money I make. He offered me a job at his store."

"And you refused it?"

"Sure. Couldn't I earn ten times as much in my own bedroom with four hours' work?"

"That is so. But you should not be seen too much with Brother Morris. He is not a loyal man, so don't give me reason to question your loyalty to me."

McMurdo was about to answer, but the door flew open, and three faces looked angrily at them from under police caps. Two guns were aimed at McMurdo's head. Another man came into the room. It was Captain Marvin, a police officer recently moved from Chicago.

"I thought you'd be getting into trouble, Mr. McMurdo of Chicago," he said. "Come with us."

"What am I charged with?" asked McMurdo.

"You are wanted in connection with the beating of old Editor Stanger."

"Well," cried McGinty with a laugh, "this man was with me at my saloon, playing cards up to midnight, and I can bring a dozen men to prove it."

"We will settle it in court tomorrow," said Marvin. "Come on, McMurdo."

He was taken to the police station and pushed into the common cell. Here he found Baldwin and three other criminals of the night before, all awaiting their trial the next morning.

But they had no cause for worry. It proved difficult to say who the attackers were due to poor light. The injured man had been so taken by surprise that he remembered nothing except that one man had a mustache. McGinty's clever lawyer was easily able to show that there was not enough evidence against the men. Brothers of the lodge smiled and waved. But there were others who sat with hate in their faces as the men walked free out of the courtroom.

Chapter 5
The Darkest Hour

Jack McMurdo's popularity increased among his fellows after the trial. But Ettie Shafter's father would have nothing more to do with him, nor would he allow him to enter the house. Ettie herself was too deeply in love to give him up completely, but she also knew she couldn't marry a criminal. She decided to go to see him, possibly for the last time.

"Give it up, Jack!" she cried, putting her arms around his neck. "For my sake, give it up!"

"How could I do it? You don't suppose that the lodge would let a man go free with all its secrets?"

"I've thought of that, Jack. Father has

saved some money. He is tired of this place where the fear of these people darkens our lives. He is ready to go. We would escape together to Philadelphia or New York, where we would be safe from them."

McMurdo laughed. "The lodge has a long arm. Do you think that they would not find us there?"

"Well then, to the West, or to England, or to Germany where father came from—anywhere to get away from this Valley of Fear!"

"I can't leave just yet, but if you give me six months, I'll work it so that we can leave here without being afraid."

The young woman laughed with joy. "Is it a promise?"

"Well, it may be seven or eight months. But within a year at the longest we will leave the valley behind us."

Ettie returned to her house more light-hearted than she had been since Jack McMurdo had come into her life.

Later that night, as the Scowrer's meeting finished, McGinty touched McMurdo on the arm and led him into the saloon's inner room.

"See here, my boy," said the Boss, "I've got a job for you at last. You can take two men with you—Manders and Reilly. You're to knock down Chester Wilcox, the head of the Iron Dike Company. Twice we've tried to get him, but had no luck, and Jim Carnaway lost his life over it. Now it's for you to try. His house is all alone on the Iron Dike road. It's no good by day because he'll see you coming. But at night, you could blow up the house using gunpowder."

"I'll do my best," promised McMurdo.

"Very good," said McGinty, shaking him by the hand.

That very night McMurdo started off to prepare for the job. It was daylight before he returned. The next day he explained his plan to Manders and Reilly, who were as excited as if it were a deer-hunt.

Two nights later they met outside the town, all three with guns and one of them carrying the gunpowder. It was two in the morning before they came to the lonely house. They moved forwards carefully with their guns in their hands.

McMurdo listened at the door of the house, but all was quiet within. He placed the gunpowder by the door and lit the fuse. Then he and his two companions ran quickly off before the house exploded into little bits.

But their well-organized work was all for nothing! Fearing for his safety, Chester Wilcox had moved himself and his family only the day before to some safer and less-known place, where a policeman could watch over them.

"Leave him to me," said McMurdo. "He's my man, and I'll get him sure if I have to wait a year for him."

Such were the ways of the Scowrers by which they spread their rule of fear over a wide district.

Chapter 6

Danger

The months went by and McMurdo was now so popular that nothing was done in the lodge without his help and advice.

It was a Saturday evening in May and McMurdo was leaving to attend the lodge meeting when Morris, the weaker brother of the order, came to see him. He looked serious and his kindly face was worried.

"I can't forget that I spoke my heart to you once, and that you kept it to yourself, even though the Boss himself came to see you about it. You are the only one I can speak to and be safe. I've got a secret, a terrible secret."

McMurdo looked at the man carefully.

"Well, let me hear it."

"There's a detective on our trail."

McMurdo stared at him in surprise. "Why, man, you're crazy," he said. "The place is full of police and detectives, and they've never done us any harm."

"No, no. It's not a man of the district. You've heard of Pinkerton's, the private detective group? If a Pinkerton man is deep in this business, we will all be destroyed."

"How did you hear of him?" asked McMurdo.

"I had a store in the East before I came here. I left good friends behind me, and one of them is in the telegram service. Here's a letter that I had from him yesterday."

McMurdo read:

How are the Scowrers in your parts? Between you and me, I heard that five big companies and two railroads have decided to plan against your group. Pinkerton's best man, Birdy Edwards, is asking a lot of questions in your area. He must be stopped immediately. I learned about this from strange messages that have come through here every day from near Vermissa.

McMurdo sat in silence for some time, with the letter in his hands. Then he suddenly jumped.

"By God!" he cried, "I've got him. We will fix this Birdy Edwards before he can do any harm. See here, Morris, will you leave this matter to me?"

"Sure, if you don't mention my name. But you won't kill this man, will you?"

"The less you know, Friend Morris, the better you will sleep."

Morris shook his head sadly as he left, feeling that he would be to blame for the detective's death.

McMurdo prepared for the worst, burning every paper which would show him to be a criminal, before he left the house. On his way to the lodge he stopped at old man Shafter's. He knocked at the window and Ettie came out to him. She read trouble in his serious face.

"Something has happened! Oh, Jack, you are in danger!"

"But it is not very bad, my love. And yet we may have to move before it is worse. I had bad news tonight, and I see trouble coming. If I go, by day or by night, you must come with me! Will you come?"

"Yes, Jack, I will come."

"Now, Ettie, it will be just a word to you, and when it reaches you, you will drop everything and come right down to the waiting room at the station."

"Day or night, I'll come when you send word, Jack."

Somewhat eased in mind, now that his own preparations for escape had begun, McMurdo went on to the lodge. The noise of pleasure and welcome greeted him as he entered. He went to his place and raised his hand.

"Eminent Bodymaster," he said in a serious

voice, taking the letter from his pocket, "I bring bad news this day. I have information that the richest and most powerful organizations in this state are planning to destroy us, and that there is a Pinkerton detective, one Birdy Edwards, at work here in Vermissa Valley. He's collecting the evidence that may put a rope around the necks of many of us, and send every man in this room into a prison cell."

There was a dead silence in the room.

"What is your evidence for this, Brother McMurdo?" the Boss asked.

"It is in this letter which has come into my hands," said McMurdo. He read the letter out loud.

"Does anyone know this Birdy Edwards by sight?" asked McGinty.

"Yes," said McMurdo, "I do."

There was a murmur of surprise through the hall.

"Eminent Bodymaster, I would ask the lodge to choose a small group, yourself, if I might suggest it, and Brother Baldwin here, and five more. To this group I can talk freely of what I know and of what I advise should be done."

The meeting finished early and left the top men to discuss the problem.

"I said just now that I knew Birdy Edwards," McMurdo explained. "Of course he is not here under that name. He passes under the name of Steve Wilson, and he is lodging at Hobson's Patch."

"How do you know him?"

"Because I talked with him once on the train—he said he was a reporter. Wanted to know all he could about the Scowrers for a New York newspaper. 'I'd pay you well,' he said 'if you could give me some information.' But I was giving nothing away."

"How did you know he wasn't a newspaper man?"

"He got out at Hobson's Patch, and so did I. I went into the telegram office, and he was leaving it.

"'See here,' said the telegram operator after Wilson had gone out. He'd filled in the form with stuff that might have been Chinese for all we could make of it. It was clearly a code. He's a detective all right."

"By God! I believe you're right," said McGinty, "but what do you think we should do about it?"

"He's in Hobson's Patch, but I don't know the house. I've got a plan, though, if you'll take my advice."

"Well, what is it?"

"I'll go over to Hobson's Patch tomorrow morning. I'll find him through the operator, then tell him I'm a Freeman myself. I'll offer him all the secrets of the lodge, for a price. I'll say the papers are at my house and tell him to come at ten o'clock at night to see everything. You can plan the rest yourselves. My house is set off the road with nothing nearby. All seven of you should come to me by nine o'clock. We'll get him!"

"At nine tomorrow we'll come," said the Boss. "Once you get the door shut behind him, you can leave the rest to us."

Chapter 7
The Trapping of Birdy Edwards

As McMurdo said, the house in which he lived was a lonely one and very well suited for such a crime as they had planned. They were hopeful that nothing of great importance had yet come to the detective's knowledge. They would find a way to make him talk before they killed him.

McMurdo went to Hobson's Patch as agreed. He was back from his trip in the afternoon, and reported to Boss McGinty at the Union House.

"I took his money, and he promised to give me much more when he has seen all my papers."

"What papers?"

"Well, there are no papers, but I lied and told him about books of rules and forms of Freeman membership. If we handle it right, they can never prove we killed him. Now, see here, Boss, I'll tell you my plan. He will come at ten and will knock three times. You will all be in the other room. I'll show him into the parlor beside the door and leave him there while I get the papers. That will give me time to tell you how things are. Then I will go back to him with some faked papers. As he is reading them, I will grab him. I'll call out and you'll rush in."

"It's a good plan," said McGinty. "The lodge will owe you for this."

When McMurdo had returned home he made his own preparations for the evening in front of him. First, he cleaned and loaded his gun. Then he discussed the matter with his housemate Scanlan. Though he was a Scowrer himself, Scanlan was secretly shocked by the actions of the lodge members, and said that he would gladly leave for the evening.

The lodge men came around nine, as

planned. On the outside they were respectable citizens, but their faces showed that there was little hope for Birdy Edwards. McGinty and Ted Baldwin were among the men who gathered that night for the killing of the Pinkerton detective. McMurdo's manner was cool, though he had planned a deadly trap for Birdy Edwards.

They all sat still. Then three loud knocks suddenly sounded at the door.

"Hush! Not a sound!" whispered McMurdo, as he went from the room, closing the door carefully behind him.

The murderers waited. Then they heard the outer door open. There were a few words of greeting. An instant later came the slam of the door and the turning of the key in the lock. He was safe within their trap. Ted Baldwin laughed, and the Boss clapped his great hand across his mouth.

"Be quiet, you fool!" he whispered.

There was the sound of conversation from the next room. Then the door opened, and McMurdo appeared, his finger on his lip.

He came to the end of the table and looked slowly around at them all. His manner had changed to that of one who has important work to do.

"Well!" cried the Boss at last. "Is he here? Is Birdy Edwards here?"

"Yes," McMurdo answered slowly. "Birdy Edwards is here. I am Birdy Edwards!"

There were ten seconds during which there was a deep silence. Seven white faces were motionless with terror. Then with a sudden breaking of glass, gun barrels broke through each window, pointing at the lodge men.

At the sight Boss McGinty gave the roar of a wounded bear and jumped for the half-opened door. A gun aiming at him and the cold blue eyes of Captain Marvin met him at the door. The Boss fell back in his chair.

"You're safer there," said the man whom they had known as McMurdo. "There are forty armed men around this house, so you have no chance. Take their guns, Marvin!" The shocked men could do nothing.

"I'd like to say a word before we separate,"

said the man who had trapped them. "You know me now for what I am. I am Birdy Edwards of Pinkerton's. I was chosen to break up your gang. It was a hard and dangerous game to play. Only Captain Marvin and my employers knew about it. But it's over tonight, thank God, and I am the winner!"

Seven pale faces looked up at him as he continued. "I never killed a man in Chicago, nor made a fake dollar in my life. But I knew the way into your good wishes, so I pretended that I was running from the law. Maybe people will say that I am as bad as you. But what is the truth? The night I joined you to beat up old man Stanger I could not warn him, but

I held your hand, Baldwin, when you would have killed him. I also gave Chester Wilcox warning, so that when I blew up his house he and his family were in hiding."

"You traitor!" cried McGinty.

"Ay, Jack McGinty, you and your likes have been the enemy of God and man in these parts. I had to stay until I had every man and every secret right here in my hand. But I had to act quickly in the end because a letter had come that would have let you know about it."

There is little more to tell. In the early morning hours, Miss Ettie Shafter and Mr. Birdy Edwards boarded a special train out of the land of danger. It was the last time that Ettie or her lover set foot in the Valley of Fear. Ten days later they were married in Chicago, with old Jacob Shafter as witness of the wedding.

The trial of the Scowrers was held far from Vermissa. McGinty was hung along with eight of his chief followers and fifty others were put in prison. The work of Birdy Edwards was complete.

And yet, the game was not over. Ted Baldwin and others were not hung and there came a day when they were freed from prison.

Birdy Edwards was chased out of Chicago after the remaining Scowrers almost killed him. He changed his name and moved to California, and it was there that the light went out in his life for a time when Ettie Edwards died. He started a business with an Englishman named Barker and made a lot of money. But again there came another warning, and he left—just in time—for England. And so he became the John Douglas who for the second time married and lived for five years as a Sussex county gentleman.

Epilogue

The trial of John Douglas finally resulted in his freedom. It was clearly self-defense, the jury found.

"Get him out of England at any cost," Holmes wrote to Mrs. Douglas. "There are forces here which may be more dangerous than those he has escaped. There is no safety for your husband in England."

Late last night our landlady brought up a message that a gentleman wished to see Holmes, and that the matter was very important. Into the

room walked Cecil Barker, our friend of the moated Manor House. His face was drawn and tired.

"I've bad news—terrible news, Mr. Holmes. It's poor Douglas. I told you that they started out for South Africa three weeks ago. The ship reached Cape Town last night. I received this telegram from Mrs. Douglas this morning:

"'Jack has been lost overboard in a storm off St. Helena. No one knows how the accident occurred.'

"'IVY DOUGLAS.'"

"So, it came like that, did it?" said Holmes thoughtfully. "Well, I've no doubt it was well planned."

"You mean you think he was murdered?" Barker asked.

"Surely!"

"Oh, those terrible Scowrers—" I started.

"No, no, my friend. This was done by Moriarty. This crime is from London, not from America."

"But for what reason?"

"I can only say that we first heard of this business through one of his associates. These Americans were well advised. They became partners with Moriarty, a great man of crime. From that moment poor Douglas had no chance."

"Don't tell me there is nothing we can do," said Barker angrily.

"No," said Holmes, and his eyes seemed to be looking far into the future. "I don't say that he can't be beat. But you must give me time—you must give me time!"

Word List

A

☐ **a ~ or two** 1～か2～、2, 3の

☐ **about** 熟 be about to まさに～しようとしている、～するところだ go on about ～をわめき散らす、～について とりとめなくしゃべる speak about ～について話す What about ~? ～についてあなたはどう思いますか。～はどうですか。

☐ **absence** 图 欠席、欠如、不在

☐ **accident** 图 ①(不慮の)事故、災難 ②偶然

☐ **according** 副《–to ~》～によれば[よると]

☐ **across** 熟 run across 走って渡る walk across ～を歩いて渡る

☐ **act** 動 ①行動する ②機能する ③演じる

☐ **activity** 图 活動、活気

☐ **actual** 形 実際の、現実の

☐ **actually** 副 実際に、本当に、実は

☐ **add** 動 ①加える、足す ②足し算をする ③言い添える

☐ **admire** 動 感心する、賞賛する

☐ **advance** 图 進歩、前進 in advance 前もって、あらかじめ

☐ **advice** 图 忠告、助言、意見

☐ **advise** 動 忠告する、勧める

☐ **affair** 图 ①事柄、事件 ②《-s》業務、仕事、やるべきこと

☐ **afraid** 熟 I'm afraid (that) 残念ながら～、悪いけれど～

☐ **Africa** 图 アフリカ《大陸》

☐ **afterward** 副 その後、のちに

☐ **afterwards** 副 その後、のちに

☐ **again and again** 何度も繰り返して

☐ **against** 熟 on guard against ~ に備えて警戒している

☐ **agent** 图 ①代理人 ②代表者

☐ **agree with** (人)に同意する

☐ **ah** 間《驚き・悲しみ・賞賛などを表して》ああ、やっぱり

☐ **aim** 動 ①(武器・カメラなどを)向ける ②ねらう、目指す

☐ **alarm** 图 ①警報、目覚まし時計 ②驚き、突然の恐怖

☐ **all** 熟 all for nothing いたずらに、無駄に all one's life ずっと、生まれてから all right 大丈夫で、よろしい、申し分ない、わかった、承知した all the way ずっと、はるばる、いろいろと at all まったく come all the way from はるばる〜からやって来る **for all** 〜〜にもかかわらず **not at all** 少しも〜でない **why this gun, of all weapons?** よりによって，なぜこの銃なのか？ **with all** 〜があ, りながら

□ **Allen, Mrs.** アレン夫人

□ **allow** 動①許す，《 − ... to 〜》…が〜するのを可能にする，…に〜させておく ②与える

□ **almanac** 名年鑑

□ **along** 熟 along with 〜と一緒に **come along** ①一緒に来る，ついて来る ②やって来る，現れる ③うまくいく，よくなる，できあがる

□ **aloud** 副大声で，(聞こえるように)声を出して

□ **altogether** 副まったく，全然，全部で

□ **America** 名アメリカ《国名・大陸》

□ **American** 形アメリカ(人)の 名アメリカ人

□ **Ames** 名エームズ《人名》

□ **ancient** 形昔の，古代の

□ **and** 熟 again and again 何度も繰り返して **and so** そこで，それだから，それで **and yet** それなのに，それにもかかわらず **over and over** 何度も繰り返して

□ **anger** 名怒り 動怒る，〜を怒らせる

□ **angrily** 副怒って，腹立たしげに

□ **any** 熟 not 〜 any longer もはや〜でない[〜しない]

□ **anyhow** 副①いずれにせよ，ともかく ②どんな方法でも

□ **anyone** 代①《疑問文・条件節で》誰か ②《否定文で》誰も (〜ない) ③《肯定文で》誰でも

□ **anything else** ほかの何か

□ **anyway** 副①いずれにせよ，ともかく ②どんな方法でも

□ **anywhere** 副どこかへ[に]，どこ

にも，どこへも，どこにでも

□ **appear** 動①現れる，見えてくる ②(〜のように)見える，〜らしい **appear to** するように見える

□ **appearance** 名①現れること，出現 ②外見，印象

□ **approach** 動①接近する ②話を持ちかける 名接近，(〜へ)近づく道

□ **armed** 形武装した

□ **around** 熟 close one's hands around the other's neck 相手の首に手を回す **come around** (人が場所を)ぶらっと訪れる **walk around** 歩き回る，ぶらぶら歩く

□ **arrange** 動①並べる，整える ②取り決める ③準備する，手はずを整える

□ **arrest** 動逮捕する 名逮捕

□ **arrive at** 〜に着く

□ **artist** 名芸術家

□ **as** 熟 as far as one can できるだけ **as for** 〜に関しては，〜はどうかと言うと **as if** あたかも〜のように，まるで〜みたいに **as to** 〜に関しては，〜については，〜に応じて **as usual** いつものように，相変わらず **as with** 〜のように，〜と同様に **see 〜 as ...** 〜を…と考える **so long as** 〜する限りは **such 〜 as ...** …のような〜

□ **aside** 副わきへ(に)，離れて **draw aside** 〜を脇へ寄せる

□ **associate** 動①連合[共同]する，提携する ②〜を連想する ③交際する 名仲間，組合員

□ **assure** 動①保障する，請け負う ②確信をもって言う

□ **at** 熟 at all まったく **at fault** 誤って，非難されるべき **at first** 最初は，初めのうちは **at last** ついに，とうとう **at once** すぐに，同時に **at some time** ある時点[時期]に **at that time** その時 **at the longest** (時間的に)長くて(も)，せいぜい **at the moment** 今は **at the most** せいぜ

い, 多くても **at the time** そのころ, 当時は **at this** これを見て, そこで (すぐに) **at work** 働いて, 仕事中で, (機械が) 稼働中で **not at all** 少しも 〜でない

□ **attack** 图 ①攻撃, 非難 ②発作, 発病

□ **attacker** 图 ①攻撃者, 敵 ②(球技の) アタッカー

□ **attend** 動 ①出席する ②世話をする, 仕える ③伴う ④《– to 〜》〜に注意を払う, 専念する, 〜の世話をする

□ **author** 图 著者, 作家

□ **await** 動 待つ, 待ち受ける

□ **away** 熟 **get away** 逃げる, 逃亡する, 離れる **give away** ①ただで与える, 贈る, 譲歩する, 手放す ②(素性・正体を) 暴露する, 馬脚を現す **take someone away** (人) を連れ出す

□ **awful** 形 ①ひどい, 不愉快な ②恐ろしい

□ **awoke** 動 awake (目覚めさせる) の過去

□ **ay** 圖 ああ, やれやれ

B

□ **back** 熟 **back in time** 過去に戻る, 時をさかのぼる **bring back** 戻す, 呼び戻す, 持ち帰る **fall back** 後退する, 退却する, 後ろ向きに倒れる **go back to** 〔場所や人の元へ〕戻る, 帰る **hold back** 〔事実・本心などを〕隠す〔秘密にする・しまっておく〕**lean back** 後ろにもたれる **push back** 押し返す, 押しのける **put back** (もとの場所に) 戻す, 返す

□ **Baker Street** ベーカー街《ロンドンの地名, ホームズとワトソンの住む家がある》

□ **Baldwin** 图 ボールドウィン《人名》

□ **Baldwin, Ted** テッド・ボールドウィン《人名》

□ **bar** 图 ①酒場 ②棒, かんぬき ③障害(物)

□ **Barker, Cecil** セシル・バーカー《人名》

□ **barrel** 图 ①たる, 1たるの分量 ②バレル《容量の単位》

□ **bear** 图 ①熊 ②(株取引で) 弱気

□ **beat** 動 ①打つ, 鼓動する ②打ち負かす

□ **beating** 图 たたくこと, 殴打

□ **beauty** 图 ①美, 美しい人 [物] ②《the –》美点

□ **because of** 〜のために, 〜の理由で

□ **bed** 熟 **go to bed** 床につく, 寝る

□ **bedroom** 图 寝室

□ **before** 熟 **the night before** 前の晩

□ **beforehand** 副 ①あらかじめ, 前もって ②早まって

□ **beg** 動 懇願する, お願いする

□ **begin with** 〜で始まる, 〜から始める

□ **behind** 前 ①〜の後ろに, 〜の背後に ②〜に遅れて, 〜に劣って 副 ①後ろに, 背後に ②遅れて, 劣って **close 〜 behind ...** …を〜の後ろで閉める **leave something behind** 残置する

□ **bell** 图 ベル, 鈴, 鐘

□ **belong** 動 《– to 〜》〜に属する, 〜のものである

□ **below** 前 ①〜より下に ②〜以下の, 〜より劣る 副 下に [へ]

□ **bent** 動 bend (曲がる) の過去, 過去分詞

□ **beside** 前 ①〜のそばに, 〜と並んで ②〜と比べると ③〜とはずれて

□ **besides** 前 ①〜に加えて, 〜のほかに ②《否定文・疑問文で》〜を除いて 副 その上, さらに

□ **best** 熟 **do one's best** 全力を尽く

す

- **between A and B** AとBの間に

- **Bible** 名 ①《the ~》聖書 ②《b-》権威ある書物, バイブル

- **bicyclist** 名 自転車乗り

- **Billy the page** ボーイのビリー

- **Birdy Edwards** バーディ・エドワーズ

- **Birlstone** 名 バールストン《地名》

- **bit** 動 bite (かむ) の過去, 過去分詞 名 ①小片, 少量 ②《a ~》少し, ちょっと

- **black-haired** 形 黒髪の

- **blame** 動 とがめる, 非難ずる

- **blew** 動 blow (吹く) の過去

- **blood** 名 ①血, 血液 ②血統, 家柄 ③気質

- **bloodmark** 名 血の跡

- **bloodstain** 名 血痕

- **blow** 動 ①(風が) 吹く, (風が) ~を吹き飛ばす ②息を吹く, (鼻を) かむ ③破裂する ④吹奏する **blow up** 破裂する [させる]

- **board** 名 宿泊と食事の提供 動 ①乗り込む ②下宿する

- **boarder** 名 下宿人

- **boarding-house** 名 宿, 下宿屋

- **Bodymaster** 名 (自由民団の) 支部長

- **boldly** 副 大胆に, 厚かましく

- **bookkeeper** 名 帳簿係

- **boot** 名 《-s》長靴, ブーツ

- **border** 名 境界, へり, 国境

- **boss** 名 上司, 親方, 監督

- **bottom** 名 ①底, 下部, すそ野, ふもと, 最下位, 根底 ②尻

- **bow** 動 (~に) お辞儀する

- **boy** 熟 **my boy** (親しい) 友達《呼びかけ》

- **brain** 名 ①脳 ②知力

- **brand** 動 ①焼き印を押す ②汚名を着せる

- **branded** 形 焼き印を押された

- **brave** 形 勇敢な

- **break through** ~を打ち破る

- **break up** ばらばらになる, 解散させる

- **breaking** 名 破壊

- **breath** 名 ①息, 呼吸 ②《a ~》(風の) そよぎ, 気配, きざし **be breath of life**〔命のように〕必要不可欠なもの

- **brightly** 副 明るく, 輝いて, 快活に

- **bring back** 戻す, 呼び戻す, 持ち帰る

- **bring down** 打ち降ろす

- **bring up** ①育てる, 連れて行く ②(問題を) 持ち出す

- **broad** 形 ①幅の広い ②寛大な ③明白な

- **brother** 名〔男性の〕同胞, 同志, 兄弟分, 同組合員 **foster brother** 乳兄弟

- **brought** 熟 Supposing that a matter were to be brought secretly to his knowledge. あることが密かに彼の知るところとなったとしよう。

- **building** 名 建物, 建造物, ビルディング

- **bundle** 名 束, 包み, 一巻き

- **burst** 動 ①爆発する [させる] ②破裂する [させる] **burst into** ~に飛び込む, 急に~する

- **bush** 名 低木, 茂み, やぶ, 未開墾地

- **busy with** 《be ~》~で忙しい

- **but** 熟 **not ~ but ...** ~ではなくて…

- **butler** 名 執事

- **by** 熟 **be taken by surprise** 意を突かれる, やみ打ちを食う **by God** 神

111

にかけて, 本当に **by day** 昼間は, 日中は **by oneself** 一人で, 自分だけで, 独力で **by the way** ところで, ついでに, 途中で **go by** ①(時が)過ぎる, 経過する ②～のそばを通る ③～に基づいて[よって]行う

C

□ **cab** 图 タクシー

□ **California** 图 カリフォルニア《米国の州》

□ **Californian** 图 カリフォルニア州の人

□ **call out** 叫ぶ, 呼び出す, 声を掛ける

□ **calm** 形 穏やかな, 落ち着いた

□ **calmly** 副 落ち着いて, 静かに

□ **can** 熟 **as far as one can** できるだけ **can do nothing** どうしようもない **can hardly** とても～できない **Can I ～?** ～してもよいですか。**Can you ～?** ～してくれますか。

□ **candle** 图 ろうそく

□ **cape** 图 岬

□ **captain** 图 長, 船長, 首領, 主将, 警部

□ **Captain Marvin** マーヴィン警部

□ **carelessly** 副 不注意にも, ぞんざいに

□ **carpet** 图 じゅうたん, 敷物 **carpet slippers** 屋内用スリッパ

□ **'cause** 略 because (～だから)の省略形

□ **cease** 動 やむ, やめる, 中止する

□ **Cecil Barker** セシル・バーカー《人名》

□ **ceiling** 图 ①天井 ②上限, 最高価格

□ **cell** 图 ①細胞 ②小区分, 小室, 独房 **common cell** 雑居房

□ **certain** 形 ①確実な, 必ず～する ②(人が)確信した ③ある ④いくらかの

□ **certainly** 副 ①確かに, 必ず ②《返答に用いて》もちろん, そのとおり, 承知しました

□ **chapter** 图 (書物の)章

□ **charge** 動 ①(代金を)請求する ②(～を…に)負わせる ③命じる

□ **charity** 图 ①慈善(行為) ②思いやり

□ **charm** 图 ①魅力, 魔力 ②まじない, お守り

□ **chase** 動 ①追跡する, 追い[探し]求める ②追い立てる

□ **check** 動 ①照合する, 検査する ②阻止[妨害]する ③(所持品を)預ける

□ **cheering** 图 歓声, 喝采

□ **chest** 图 ①大きな箱, 戸棚, たんす ②金庫 ③胸, 肺

□ **Chester Wilcox** チェスター・ウィルコック《人名》

□ **Chicago** 图 シカゴ《地名》

□ **chief** 图 頭, 長, 親分 形 最高位の, 第一の, 主要な

□ **chill** 图 冷え, 身にしみる寒さ

□ **chin** 图 あご

□ **Chinese** 形 中国(人)の 图 ①中国人 ②中国語

□ **cipher** 图 暗号文

□ **circle** 图 ①円, 円周, 輪 ②循環, 軌道 ③仲間, サークル

□ **citizen** 图 ①市民, 国民 ②住民, 民間人

□ **clap** 動 (手を)たたく

□ **clean-shaven** 形 ひげのない

□ **clear** 形 ①はっきりした, 明白な ②澄んだ ③(よく)晴れた

□ **clearly** 副 ①明らかに, はっきりと ②《返答に用いて》そのとおり

□ **clever** 形 ①頭のよい, 利口な ②器

用な, 上手な

□ **close to** 《be –》〜に近い

□ **close ~ behind ...** …を〜の後ろで閉める

□ **close one's hands around the other's neck** 相手の首に手を回す

□ **closely** 副①密接に ②念入りに, 詳しく ③ぴったりと

□ **clothing** 名衣類, 衣料品

□ **clue** 名手がかり, 糸口

□ **coal** 名石炭, 木炭

□ **coal-mining town** 炭鉱町

□ **code** 名①法典 ②規準, 慣例 ③コート, 番号 secret code 暗号

□ **coded message** 暗号(化された)メッセージ, 暗号文

□ **coldly** 副冷たく, よそよそしく

□ **column** 名①コラム ②(新聞などの)縦の段[行・列] ③(円)柱 double column 2段組み

□ **come** 熟 come all the way from はるばる〜からやって来る come along ①一緒に来る, ついて来る ②やって来る, 現れる ③うまくいく, よくなる, できあがる come around 〔人が場所を〕ぶらっと訪れる come down 下りて来る, 田舎へ来る come in 中にはいる, やってくる, 出回る come into 〜に入ってくる come into someone's life (人)の人生に入り込む[関わる] come on ①いいかげんにしろ, もうよせ, さあ来なさい ②(人)に偶然出合う come out 出てくる, 出掛ける, 姿を現す, 発行される come out of 〜から出てくる, 〜をうまく乗り越える come through 通り抜ける, 成功する, 期待に沿う come to no harm 危害を受けない, ひどい目に遭わない come up 近づいてくる, 階上に行く, 浮上する, 水面へ上ってくる, 発生する, 芽を出す come up with 〜に行きつく if it comes to 〜のことになると, 〜に関して言えば

□ **comfortable** 形快適な, 心地いい

□ **commercial** 名コマーシャル Eagle Commercial イーグル・コマーシャル《ホテル名》

□ **common** 熟 common cell 雑居房 in common use《be 〜》一般的に使われて[用いられて]いる

□ **companion** 名①友, 仲間, 連れ ②添えもの, つきもの

□ **complete** 形完全な, まったくの, 完成した

□ **completely** 副完全に, すっかり

□ **concern** 動①関係する, 《be -ed in [with] 〜》〜に関係している ②心配させる, 《be -ed about [for] 〜》〜を心配する

□ **concert** 名①音楽[演奏]会, コンサート ②一致, 協力

□ **confident-looking** 形自信に満ちて見える

□ **connect** 動つながる, つなぐ, 関係づける

□ **connection** 名①つながり, 関係 ②縁故

□ **consider** 動①考慮する, 〜しようと思う ②(〜と)みなす ③気にかける, 思いやる

□ **control** 動①管理[支配]する ②抑制する, コントロールする 名①管理, 支配(力) in control 〜を支配している, 〜を掌握している

□ **conversation** 名会話, 会談

□ **cop** 名警官

□ **cord** 名ひも, コード

□ **cost** 名①値段, 費用 ②損失, 犠牲

□ **could** 熟 could have done 〜だったかもしれない《仮定法》 Could I 〜?〜してもよいですか。 Could you 〜?〜してくださいますか。 How could 〜?何だって〜なんてことがありえようか? If +《主語》+ could 〜できればなあ《仮定法》

□ **count** 動①数える ②(〜を…と)みなす ③重要[大切]である

□ **countryside** 名地方, 田舎

□ **county** 名郡, 州

□ **couple** 名①2つ, 対 ②夫婦, 一組 ③数個 a couple of 2, 3の

□ **course** 熟 of course もちろん, 当然

□ **court** 名①中庭, コート ②法廷, 裁判所 ③宮廷, 宮殿

□ **courtroom** 名法廷

□ **cover** 名覆い, カバー

□ **crazy** 形①狂気の, ばかげた, 無茶な ②夢中の, 熱狂的な

□ **crime** 名①(法律上の)罪, 犯罪 ②悪事, よくない行為

□ **criminal** 形犯罪の, 罪深い, 恥ずべき 名犯罪者, 犯人

□ **crook** 動曲げる, 湾曲する

□ **crowd** 名群集, 雑踏, 多数, 聴衆 push one's way through the crowd 人混みの中を押し分けて進む

□ **crowded** 形混雑した, 満員の

□ **cry out** 叫ぶ

□ **curious** 形好奇心の強い, 珍しい, 奇妙な, 知りたがる

□ **current** 形現在の, 目下の, 通用[流通]している

□ **curse** 動のろう, ののしる Curse you. この野郎。

□ **curved** 形曲がった, 湾曲した

□ **cut-off** 名切り離すこと

□ **cutting** 名①切ること, 裁断, カッティング ②(新聞などの)切り抜き, (挿し木用の)切り枝

□ **cycle** 名①周期, 循環 ②自転車, オートバイ

D

□ **dare** 動《– to 〜》思い切って[あえて]〜する

□ **dark** 熟 get dark 暗くなる

□ **darken** 動暗くする[なる]

□ **darkness** 名暗さ, 暗やみ

□ **dawning** 名始まりの, 夜明けの

□ **day** 熟 by day 昼間は, 日中は every day 毎日

□ **daylight** 名①日光, 昼の明かり, 昼間 ②夜明け

□ **dazed** 形放心状態の, ぼうぜんとした

□ **deadly** 形命にかかわる, 痛烈な, 破壊的な

□ **deaf** 形耳が聞こえない

□ **dealing** 名取引

□ **Dear me** おや!, まあ!《驚きを表す》

□ **death** 名①死, 死ぬこと ②《the –》終えん, 消滅 put the fear of death into (人)をひどく怖がらせる, (人)をびびらせる

□ **decide to do** 〜することに決める

□ **deeply** 副深く, 非常に

□ **deer-hunt** 名鹿狩りをすること

□ **delight** 名喜び, 愉快

□ **demand** 動①要求する, 尋ねる ②必要とする

□ **departure** 名①出発, 発車 ②離脱

□ **depend** 動《– on [upon] 〜》①〜を頼る, 〜をあてにする ②〜による

□ **describe** 動(言葉で)描写する, 特色を述べる, 説明する

□ **description** 名(言葉で)記述(すること), 描写(すること)

□ **design** 名デザイン, 設計(図)

□ **destroy** 動破壊する, 絶滅させる, 無効にする

114

□ **detail** 名①細部,《-s》詳細 ②《-s》個人情報

□ **detective** 名探偵,刑事

□ **difficulty** 名①むずかしさ ②難局,支障,苦情,異議 ③《-ties》財政困難

□ **dining** 名食事,夕食をとること **dining room** 食堂

□ **directly** 副①じかに ②まっすぐに ③ちょうど

□ **dirty** 形①汚い,汚れた ②卑劣な,不正な

□ **discourse** 動話をする

□ **discuss** 動議論[検討]する

□ **disobey** 動服従しない,違反する

□ **distant** 形①遠い,隔たった ②よそよそしい,距離のある

□ **district** 名①地方,地域 ②行政区

□ **do** 熟 **can do nothing** どうしようもない **do one's best** 全力を尽くす **do with** ～を処理する

□ **door** 熟 **knock on the door** ドアをノックする

□ **double** 形①2倍の,二重の ②対の **double column** 2段組み

□ **doubt** 名①疑い,不確かなこと ②未解決点,困難 動疑う **no doubt** きっと,たぶん

□ **Douglas, John** ジョン・ダグラス《人名》

□ **Douglas, Mrs.** ダグラス夫人

□ **down** 熟 **bring down** 打ち降ろす **come down** 下りて来る,田舎へ来る **go down** 下に降りる,下りる **go down to** ～に出かける,～に赴く **hurry down** 急いで下りる[駆け込む] **look down** 見下ろす **put down** 下に置く,下ろす **rush down** 猛然と～に駆け寄る **settle down** 落ち着く,興奮がおさまる **strike down**(人)を打ち倒す,(人)を殺す **throw down** 投げ出す,放棄する **weigh ～ down**〔重さで〕垂れ下がらせる **write down** 書き留める

□ **downstairs** 副階下で,下の部屋で 形階下の

□ **dozen** 名1ダース,12(個)

□ **Dr.** 名～博士,《医者に対して》～先生

□ **drag** 動①引きずる ②のろのろ動く[動かす]

□ **drain** 動①(水が)流れる ②(水が)引く ③水抜きをする,排出させる

□ **drama** 名劇,演劇,ドラマ,劇的な事件

□ **draw** 動①引く,引っ張る ②描く ③引き分けになる[する] **draw aside** ～を脇へ寄せる **draw out** 引き抜く

□ **drawbridge** 名跳ね橋

□ **drawn** 動draw(引く)の過去分詞

□ **dressing** 名①ドレッシング ②着付け,衣装 ③手当て,手入れ,下ごしらえ

□ **dressing gown** ドレッシングガウン《コートのように長くてゆったりした部屋着》

□ **dressing room** 更衣室

□ **drew** 動draw(引く)の過去

□ **due** 形予定された,期日のきている,支払われるべき **due to** ～によって,・が原因で

□ **dumb-bell** 名ダンベル,鉄アレイ

E

□ **eagerly** 副熱心に,しきりに

□ **eagle** 名ワシ(鷲)

□ **Eagle Commercial** イーグル・コマーシャル《ホテル名》

□ **earn** 動①儲ける,稼ぐ ②(名声を)博す

□ **earth** 熟 **on earth** ①いったい ②地球上で,この世で

□ **ease** 動安心させる,楽にする,ゆる

める

□ **easily** 副①容易に, たやすく, 苦もなく ②気楽に

□ **editor** 名編集者, 編集長

□ **effect** 名①影響, 効果, 結果 ②実施, 発効

□ **else** 熟anything else ほかの何か

□ **eminent** 形 (身分などが) 高い, 名高い, 高名な

□ **employer** 名雇主, 使用[利用]する人

□ **encourage** 動①勇気づける ②促進する, 助長する

□ **end** 熟in the end とうとう, 結局, ついに

□ **endure** 動①我慢する, 耐え忍ぶ ②持ちこたえる

□ **enemy** 名敵

□ **England** 名①イングランド ②英国

□ **Englishman** 名イングランド人, イギリス人

□ **enjoy doing** ～するのが好きだ, ～するのを楽しむ

□ **enough** 熟enough of ～はもうたくさん enough to do ～するのに十分な sure enough 思ったとおり, 案の定

□ **entirely** 副完全に, まったく

□ **epilogue** 名①(劇の) 納め口上, エピローグ ②終章, 終節

□ **escape** 動逃げる, 免れる, もれる 名逃亡, 脱出, もれ

□ **Ettie Shafter** エティー・シャフター《人名》

□ **even though** ～であるけれども, ～にもかかわらず

□ **every day** 毎日

□ **everyone** 代誰でも, 皆

□ **everything** 代すべてのこと[もの], 何でも, 何もかも

□ **evidence** 名①証拠, 証人 ②形跡

□ **evil** 名①邪悪 ②害, わざわい, 不幸

□ **examine** 動試験する, 調査[検査]する, 診察する

□ **excellent** 形優れた, 優秀な

□ **except** 前～を除いて, ～のほかは 接～ということを除いて except for ～を除いて, ～がなければ

□ **excited** 形興奮した, わくわくした

□ **excitedly** 副興奮して

□ **excitement** 名興奮 (すること)

□ **exclaim** 動①(喜び・驚きなどで) 声をあげる ②声高に激しく言う

□ **exist** 動存在する, 生存する, ある, いる

□ **expect** 動予期[予測]する, (当然のこととして) 期待する

□ **explanation** 名①説明, 解説, 釈明 ②解釈, 意味

□ **explode** 動①爆発する[させる] ②(感情が) ほとばしる, 突然～し出す

F

□ **fail** 名失敗, 落第点 without fail 必ず, 確実に

□ **fair** 形①正しい, 公平[正当]な ②快晴の ③色白の, 金髪の ④かなりの ⑤《古》美しい

□ **fair-haired** 形金髪の

□ **fake** 形にせの

□ **faked** 形捏造した faked paper 偽札

□ **fall** 熟fall back 後退する, 戻る, 退却する, 後ろ向きに倒れる let fall 〔言葉を〕うっかり漏らす[しゃべる]

□ **far** 熟as far as one can できるだけ far from ～から遠い, ～どころか far into ずっと far side 向こう側, 反対側 so far 今までのところ, これまでは

□ **farmer** 图 農民, 農場経営者

□ **fault** 图 ①欠点, 短所 ②過失, 誤り **at fault** 誤って, 非難されるべき **be at fault for** 〜に対して責任がある

□ **fear** 图 ①恐れ ②心配, 不安 動 ① 恐れる ②心配する **put the fear of death into** (人)をひどく怖がらせる, (人)をびびらせる **rule of fear** 恐怖 による支配 **with fear** 怖がって

□ **feel** 熟 **feel like** 〜がほしい, 〜し たい気がする, 〜のような感じがする **not feel like doing** 〜する気になれ ない

□ **feeling** 動 feel(感じる)の現在分 詞 图 ①感じ, 気持ち ②触感, 知覚 ③同情 思いやり 感受性

□ **feet** 熟 **jump to one's feet** 飛び起 きる **on one's feet** 立っている状態 で **to one's feet** 両足で立っている 状態に

□ **fellow** 图 ①仲間, 同僚 ②人, やつ 形 仲間の, 同士の

□ **fever** 图 ①熱, 熱狂 ②熱病

□ **field** 熟 **gold field** 金鉱

□ **figure** 图 ①人[物]の姿, 形 ②図 (形) ③数字

□ **fill in** 〜に記入する

□ **filled with** 《be 〜》〜でいっぱい になる

□ **final** 形 最後の, 決定的な

□ **firm** 图 会社, 事務所

□ **firmly** 副 しっかりと, 断固として

□ **first** 熟 **at first** 最初は, 初めのうち は

□ **firstly** 副 初めに, まず第一に

□ **fishing** 图 釣り, 魚業

□ **fit** 動 合致[適合]する, 合致させる **fit in with** 〜に適合する

□ **fix** 動 ①固定する[させる] ②修理 する ③決定する ④用意する, 整える ⑤〔人を〕殺す, 片付ける, 仕留める

□ **floor** 熟 **ground floor** 〈英〉1階

□ **folk** 图 ①(生活様式を共にする) 人々 ②《one's -s》家族, 親類

□ **follower** 图 信奉者, 追随者

□ **following** 動 follow(ついていく) の現在分詞 形 《the 〜》次の, 次に続 く

□ **fool** 图 ①ばか者, おろかな人 ②道 化師

□ **footmark** 图 足跡

□ **for** 熟 **for a moment** 少しの間 **for a time** しばらく, 一時の間 **for a while** しばらくの間, 少しの間 **for all 〜** 〜にもかかわらず **for god's sake** 一生のお願いだから, どうかお 願いだから **for life** 死ぬまでずっと **for nothing** ただで, 無料で, むだに **for now** 今のところ, ひとまず **for oneself** 独力で, 自分のために **for some time** しばらくの間 **for the moment** 差し当たり, 当座は **for 〜 years** 〜年間, 〜年にわたって

□ **force** 图 力, 勢い 動 ①強制する, 力ずくで〜する, 余儀なく〜させる ②押しやる, 押し込む

□ **forgive** 動 許す, 免除する

□ **forgiven** 動 forgive(許す)の過去 分詞

□ **form** 图 ①形, 形式 ②書式

□ **formal** 形 正式の, 公式の, 形式的な, 格式ばった

□ **forward** 副 ①前方に ②将来に向 けて ③先へ, 進んで

□ **frame** 图 骨組み, 構造, 額縁

□ **Fred Porlock** フレッド・ポーロ ック《人名》

□ **free** 熟 **go free** 自由の身になる

□ **freedom** 图 ①自由 ②束縛がない こと

□ **freely** 副 自由に, 障害なしに

□ **freeman** 图 自由民団の一員

□ **freemen** 图 freeman(自由民団の 一員)の複数 **Order of Freemen** 自 由民団

□ **French** 形 フランス（人・語）の 名 ①フランス語 ②《the –》フランス人

□ **frequent** 形 ひんぱんな、よくある

□ **friend of mine** 《a –》友人の1人

□ **friendly** 形 親しみのある、親切な、友情のこもった

□ **friendship** 名 友人であること、友情

□ **frightened** 形 おびえた、びっくりした

□ **frightening** 形 恐ろしい、どきっとさせる

□ **from now** 今から、これから

□ **from ~ to ...** ～から…まで

□ **front** 熟 in front of ～の前に、～の正面に

□ **full of** 《be –》～で一杯である

□ **fully** 副 十分に、完全に、まるまる

□ **further** 形 いっそう遠い、その上の、なおいっそうの、副 いっそう遠く、その上に、もっと

□ **fuse** 名 （電気の）ヒューズ、信管、導火線

G

□ **gain** 動 ①得る、増す ②進歩する、進む

□ **gang** 名 ①群れ、一団 ②ギャング、暴力団 ③（子ども、若者の）遊び仲間、非行少年グループ

□ **gateway** 名 出入り口、道

□ **gather** 動 ①集まる、集める ②生じる、増す ③推測する

□ **German** 形 ドイツ（人・語）の 名 ①ドイツ人 ②ドイツ語

□ **Germany** 名 ドイツ《国名》

□ **get** 熟 get a job 職を得る get away 逃げる、逃亡する、離れる get

dark 暗くなる get hold of ～を手に入れる、～をつかむ get home 家に着く[帰る] get in 中に入る、乗り込む get into ～に入る、入り込む、～に巻き込まれる get into trouble 面倒を起こす、困った事になる、トラブルに巻き込まれる get off （～から）降りる get out ①外に出る、出て行く、逃げ出す ②取り出す、抜き出す get started 始める get to （事）を始める、～に達する[到着する]

□ **giant** 名 ①巨人、大男 ②巨匠

□ **give away** ①ただで与える、贈る、譲歩する、手放す ②（素性・正体を）暴露する、馬脚を現す

□ **give someone a lesson** （人）に教訓を与える、（人）を懲らしめる

□ **give up** あきらめる、やめる、引き渡す

□ **glad to do** 《be –》～してうれしい、喜んで～する

□ **gladly** 副 喜んで、うれしそうに

□ **glance** 動 ①ちらりと見る ②かすめる

□ **glow** 名 ①白熱、輝き ②ほてり、熱情

□ **go** 熟 go back to ［場所や人の元へ］戻る、帰る go by ①（時が）過ぎる、経過する ②～のそばを通る ③～に基づいて[よって]行う go down 下に行く、下りる go down to ～に出かける、～に赴く go free 自由の身になる go home 帰宅する go in 中に入る、開始する go into ～に入る、（仕事）に就く go on about ～をわめき散らす、～についてとりとめなくしゃべる go on one's way 道を進む、立ち去る go on to ～に移る、～に取り掛かる go out 外出する、外へ出る、消灯する go over to ～の前に[へ]行く、～に出向いて行く go round ～の周りを進む、歩き回る、回って行く go to bed 床につく、寝る go with ～と一緒に行く let go 手を放す、行かせる ready to go すっかり準備が整った

118

□ **god** 熟 by God 神にかけて, 本当に for god's sake 一生のお願いだから, どうかお願いだから Thank God. ありがたい

□ **gold** 名金, 金貨, 金製品, 金色 形金の, 金製の, 金色の

□ **gold field** 金鉱

□ **good** 熟 good wishes 好意, 厚情 take a good look at ～をよく見る

□ **gotten** 動 get（得る）の過去分詞

□ **gown** 名ガウン, 室内着 dressing gown ドレッシングガウン《コートのように長くてゆったりした部屋着》

□ **grab** 動①ふいにつかむ, ひったくる ②横取りする

□ **gray-haired** 形白髪頭の

□ **grayish** 形灰色がかった

□ **greatly** 副大いに

□ **greet** 動①あいさつする ②（喜んで）迎える

□ **greeting** 名あいさつ（の言葉）, あいさつ（状）

□ **ground floor** 〈英〉1階

□ **guard** 名①警戒, 見張り ②番人 動番をする, 監視する, 守る be on one's guard 気を付ける, 警戒する on guard against ～に備えて警戒している on one's guard〔危険・敵などに対して〕警戒［用心・注意］する

□ **guilt** 名罪, 有罪, 犯罪

□ **guilty** 形有罪の, やましい

□ **gun** 名銃, 大砲 why this gun, of all weapons? よりによって, なぜこの銃なのか？

□ **gunpowder** 名火薬

□ **gunshot** 名射撃, 発砲

H

□ **ha** 間ほう, まあ, おや《驚き・悲しみ・不満・喜び・笑い声などを表す》

□ **habit** 名習慣, 癖, 気質

□ **half-opened** 形半開の

□ **half-past** 副～時半すぎ

□ **halfway** 副中間［中途］で, 不完全に halfway up 半ばまで上った所に

□ **hall** 名公会堂, ホール, 大広間, 玄関

□ **Hampstead** 名ハムステッド《地名》

□ **hand** 熟 close one's hands around the other's neck 相手の首に手を回す rule ～ with a heavy hand ～を厳しく統治［支配］する shake hands 握手をする

□ **handle** 動①手を触れる ②操縦する, 取り扱う

□ **handsome** 形端正な（顔立ちの）, りっぱな,（男性が）ハンサムな

□ **hang** 動かかる, かける, つるす, ぶら下がる hang over〔危険が〕差し迫る, ～を脅かす

□ **happen to** たまたま～する, 偶然～する

□ **happening** 名出来事, 事件

□ **hard of hearing** 耳の不自由な, 耳が遠い［よく聞こえない］

□ **hard to** ～し難い

□ **hard-looking** 形厳しい, 荒々しい, 無慈悲な

□ **hardly** 副①ほとんど～でない, わずかに ②厳しく, かろうじて can hardly とても～できない

□ **Hargrave** 名ハーグレイヴ《人名》

□ **harm** 名害, 損害 come to no harm 危害を受けない, ひどい目に遭わない

□ **hate** 動嫌う, 憎む,（～するのを）いやがる 名憎しみ

□ **have** 熟 could have done ～だったかもしれない《仮定法》have a talk 話をする have no idea わからない have someone in（人）を家に呼ぶ

□ **head of** ～の長

119

□ **hear of** 〜について聞く

□ **hearing** 動 hear (聞く)の現在分詞 名 ①聞くこと, 聴取, 聴力 ②聴聞会, ヒアリング **hard of hearing** 耳の不自由な, 耳が遠い[よく聞こえない]

□ **heart** 熟 **win someone's heart** (人)のハートを射止める

□ **heaven** 名 ①天国 ②天国のようなところ[状態], 楽園 ③空 ④〈H-〉神

□ **heavy** 熟 **rule 〜 with a heavy hand** 〜を厳しく統治[支配]する

□ **height** 名 ①高さ, 身長 ②《the -》絶頂, 真っ盛り ③高台, 丘

□ **Helena, St.** セントヘレナ《島名》

□ **hell** 名 地獄, 地獄のようなところ[状態]

□ **help 〜 to ...** 〜が…するのを助ける

□ **herald** 名 ①使者, 伝達者, 報道者 ②先駆者

□ **Herald** 名 《ヴァーミッサ・》ヘラルド《新聞(社)の名》

□ **here is 〜** こちらは〜です。

□ **hid** 動 hide (隠れる)の過去, 過去分詞

□ **hidden** 動 hide (隠れる)の過去分詞

□ **hide** 動 隠れる, 隠す, 隠れて見えない, 秘密にする

□ **hiding** 名 隠す[隠れる]こと

□ **hint** 名 暗示, ヒント, 気配

□ **Hobson's Patch** ホブソンズ・パッチ《地名》

□ **hold** 熟 **get hold of** 〜を手に入れる, 〜をつかむ **hold back** [事実・本心などを]隠す[秘密にする・しまっておく] **hold in** (動かないように)押さえる **hold out** ①差し出す, (腕を)伸ばす ②持ちこたえる, 粘る, 耐える

□ **Holmes, Sherlock** シャーロック・ホームズ《人名》

□ **home** 熟 **get home** 家に着く[帰る] **go home** 帰宅する

□ **honor** 名 ①名誉, 光栄, 信用 ②節操, 自尊心 動 尊敬する, 栄誉を与える

□ **hopeful** 形 希望に満ちた, 望みを抱いて(いる), 有望な

□ **horror** 名 ①恐怖, ぞっとすること ②嫌悪

□ **host** 名 ①客をもてなす主人 ②(テレビなどの)司会者

□ **house** 熟 **manor house** [荘園の]領主の館[邸宅]

□ **household** 名 家族, 世帯

□ **housekeeper** 名 家政婦

□ **housemate** 名 同居人

□ **How could 〜?** 何だって〜なんてことがあるだろうか?

□ **how to 〜** する方法

□ **however** 接 けれども, だが

□ **huge** 形 巨大な, ばく大な

□ **hullo** 間 やあ, おや

□ **humble** 形 つつましい, 粗末な

□ **humor** 名 ①ユーモア ②(一時的な)機嫌

□ **humorous** 形 こっけいな, ユーモアのある

□ **hung** 動 hang (かかる)の過去, 過去分詞

□ **hurry down** 急いで下りる[駆け込む]

□ **hush** 間 しっ! 静かに!

I

□ **I'm afraid (that)** 残念ながら〜, 悪いけれど〜

□ **idea** 熟 **have no idea** わからない

□ **identify** 動 ①(本人・同一と)確認

120

する, 見分ける ②意気投合する

- □ **if** 熟 **as if** あたかも〜のように, まるで〜みたいに **if it comes to** 〜のことになると, 〜に関して言えば **if you please** よろしければ **If +《主語》+ could** 〜できればなあ《仮定法》 **see if** 〜かどうかを確かめる, 〜かどうかを見る **what if** もし〜だったらどうなるだろうか

- □ **imagine** 動 想像する, 心に思い描く

- □ **immediately** 副 すぐに, 〜するやいなや

- □ **importance** 名 重要性, 大切さ

- □ **impress** 動 印象づける, 感銘させる

- □ **in** 熟 **in a moment** ただちに **in advance** 前もって, あらかじめ **in an instant** たちまち, ただちに **in common use**《be 〜》一般的に使われて[用いられて]いる **in control** 〜を支配して, 〜を掌握している **in front of** 〜の前に, 〜の正面に **in peace** 平和のうちに, 安心して **in silence** 黙って, 沈黙のうちに **in some way** 何とかして, 何らかの方法で **in such a way** そのような方法で **in the end** とうとう, 結局, ついに **in the world** 世界で **in touch** 連絡を取って **in trouble** 面倒な状況で, 困って

- □ **inch** 名 ①インチ《長さの単位。1/12フィート, 2.54cm》②少量

- □ **income** 名 収入, 所得, 収益

- □ **increase** 動 増加[増強]する, 増やす, 増える

- □ **indecision** 名 優柔不断, ためらい

- □ **indeed** 副 ①実際, 本当に ②《強意》まったく

- □ **injured** 形 負傷した, (名誉・感情などを)損ねられた

- □ **ink** 名 インク

- □ **inner** 形 ①内部の ②心の中の

- □ **inquire** 動 尋ねる, 問う

- □ **inspect** 動 検査する, 調べる

- □ **inspector** 名 ①検査する人 ②(英国の)警部補

- □ **Inspector MacDonald** マクドナルド警部補

- □ **instant** 形 即時の, 緊急の, 即席の 名 瞬間, 寸時 **in an instant** たちまち, ただちに

- □ **instantly** 副 すぐに, 即座に

- □ **instruct** 動 ①教える, 教育する ②指図[命令]する

- □ **intend** 動《 – to 〜》〜しようと思う, 〜するつもりである

- □ **interested** 形 興味を持った, 関心のある

- □ **interesting** 形 おもしろい, 興味を起こさせる

- □ **interrupt** 動 さえぎる, 妨害する, 口をはさむ

- □ **into** 熟 **burst into** 〜に飛び込む, 急に〜する **come into** 〜に入ってくる **far into** ずっと **get into** 〜に入る, 入り込む, 〜に巻き込まれる **get into trouble** 面倒を起こす, 困った事になる, トラブルに巻き込まれる **go into** 〜に入る, (仕事)に就く **lead into** (ある場所)へ導く **look into** ①〜を検討する, 〜を研究する ②の中を見る, 〜をのぞき込む **make one's way into** 〔部屋など〕に入る **put 〜 into ...** 〜を…の状態にする, 〜を…に突っ込む **put the fear of death into** (人)をひどく怖がらせる, (人)をびびらせる

- □ **investigate** 動 研究する, 調査する, 捜査する

- □ **investigation** 名 (徹底的な)調査, 取り調べ

- □ **Ireland** 名 アイルランド《国名》

- □ **Irishman** 名 アイルランド(系)人

- □ **iron** 名 ①鉄, 鉄製のもの ②アイロン 形 鉄の, 鉄製の

- □ **Iron Dike Company** アイアン・ダイク・カンパニー《会社名》

A
B
C
D
E
F
G
H
I
J
K
L
M
N
O
P
Q
R
S
T
U
V
W
X
Y
Z

□ **Iron Dike road** アイアン・ダイク道路

□ **It is ~ for someone to ...** (人)が…するのは～だ

□ **ivy** 名ツタ(蔦), つる植物

□ **Ivy Douglas** アイビー・ダグラス《人名》

J

□ **Jack McGinty** ジャック・マギンティ《人名》

□ **Jack McMurdo** ジャック・マクマードー《人名》

□ **jacket** 名①短い上着 ②(書物などの)カバー

□ **Jacob Shafter** ジェイコブ・シャフター《人名》

□ **James Stanger** ジェームズ・スタンジャー《人名》

□ **jaw** 名①あご ②《-s》あご状のもの

□ **jealousy** 名嫉妬, ねたみ

□ **Jean Baptiste Greuze** ジャン=バティスト・グルーズ《フランスの画家, 1725-1805》

□ **Jim Carnaway** ジム・カーナウェイ《人名》

□ **job** 熟get a job 職を得る

□ **John Douglas** ジョン・ダグラス《人名》

□ **joke** 名冗談, ジョーク

□ **Jonas Pinto** ジョナス・ピント《人名》

□ **journey** 名①(遠い目的地への)旅 ②行程

□ **joy** 名喜び, 楽しみ

□ **jump to one's feet** 飛び起きる

□ **jury** 名①陪審, 陪審員団 ②(展示会・競技会などの)審査員団, 調査委員会

□ **just in time** いよいよというとき

に, すんでのところで, やっと間に合って

K

□ **keep up** 続ける, 続く, 維持する, (遅れないで)ついていく, 上げたままにしておく

□ **keeper** 名保護者, 後見人

□ **killer** 名殺人者[犯]

□ **killing** 名殺害, 殺人

□ **kind of** ある程度, いくらか, ～のようなもの[人]

□ **kind-looking** 形親切そうな

□ **kindly** 形①親切な, 情け深い, 思いやりのある ②(気候などの)温和な, 快い

□ **kiss** 動キスする

□ **knife** 名ナイフ, 小刀, 包丁, 短剣

□ **knock** 動ノックする, たたく, ぶつける 名打つこと, 戸をたたくこと[音] knock on the door ドアをノックする

□ **know** 熟know nothing of ～のことを知らない know of ～について知っている you know ご存知のとおり, そうでしょう

□ **knowledge** 名知識, 理解, 学問 Supposing that a matter were to be brought secretly to his knowledge. あることが密かに彼の知るところとなったとしよう。

□ **known to** 《be ‒》～に知られている

L

□ **laid** 動lay (置く)の過去, 過去分詞

□ **lamp** 名ランプ, 灯火

□ **landlady** 名女家主, 女主人

□ **last** 熟at last ついに, とうとう

the last time この前〜したとき

□ **latest** 形 ①最新の, 最近の ②最も遅い

□ **laughter** 名 笑い(声)

□ **law and order** 治安, 法と秩序

□ **lawless** 形 ①法律のない, 不法な ②無法な, 手に負えない

□ **lawyer** 名 弁護士, 法律家

□ **lay** 動 ①置く, 横たえる, 敷く ②整える ③卵を産む ④lie(横たわる)の過去

□ **lead** 名 糸口, 手掛かり lead into (ある場所)へ導く lead to 〜に至る, 〜に通じる, 〜を引き起こす

□ **leading** 形 主要な, 指導的な, 先頭の

□ **lean** 動 ①もたれる, 寄りかかる ②傾く, 傾ける lean back 後ろにもたれる lean over 〜にかがみ込む

□ **leave** 熟 leave for 〜に向かって出発する leave something behind 残置する make someone leave 退校[職]させる

□ **led** 動 lead(導く)の過去, 過去分詞

□ **length** 名 長さ, 縦, たけ, 距離

□ **less** 副 〜より少なく, 〜ほどでなく less likely to 〜する傾向が弱い[可能性が低い] no less やはり, 同様に

□ **less-known** 形 あまり知られていない

□ **lesson** 熟 give someone a lesson (人)に教訓を与える, (人)を懲らしめる

□ **let fall** 〔言葉を〕うっかり漏らす[しゃべる]

□ **let go** 手を放す, 行かせる

□ **let us** どうか私たちに〜させてください

□ **lettering** 名 書いた[刻んだ]文字, 銘

□ **lie** 動 ①うそをつく ②横たわる, 寝る ③(ある状態に)ある, 存在する 名 うそ, 詐欺

□ **life** 熟 all one's life ずっと, 生まれてから be breath of life〔命のように〕必要不可欠なもの come into someone's life (人)の人生に入り込む[関わる] for life 死ぬまでずっと

□ **light-hearted** 形 気楽な, 快活な

□ **like** 熟 feel like 〜がほしい, 〜したい気がする, 〜のような感じがする look like 〜のように見える, 〜に似ている not feel like doing 〜する気になれない would like 〜がほしい would like to 〜したいと思う

□ **likely** 形 ①ありそうな, (〜)しそうな ②適当な less likely to 〜する傾向が弱い[可能性が低い] not likely ありそうもない, 可能性が低い very likely たぶん

□ **lip** 名 唇, 《-s》口

□ **lit** 動 light(火をつける)の過去, 過去分詞

□ **living** 動 live(住む)の現在分詞

□ **loaded** 動 load(積む)の過去, 過去分詞 形 荷を積んだ, 詰め込んだ

□ **lodge** 名 ①番小屋, 山小屋 ②〔組合などの組織の〕支部

□ **London** 名 ロンドン《英国の首都》

□ **lonely** 形 ①孤独な, 心さびしい ②ひっそりした, 人里離れた

□ **long** 熟 so long as 〜する限りは

□ **longer** 熟 no longer もはや〜でない[〜しない] not 〜 any longer もはや〜でない[〜しない]

□ **longest** 熟 at the longest (時間的に)長くて(も), せいぜい.

□ **look** 熟 look down 見下ろす look for 〜を探す look in 中を見る, 立ち寄る look into 〜を検討する, 〜を研究する ②〜の中を見る, 〜をのぞき込む look like 〜のように見える, 〜に似ている look out ①外を見る ②気をつける, 注意する look out of (窓などから)外を見る look up 見上げる, 調べる take a good look at 〜をよく見る

123

□ **lot of** 《a-》たくさんの〜

□ **love** 國 be in love with 〜に恋して、〜に心を奪われて

□ **lover** 图 ①愛人、恋人 ②愛好者

□ **loving** 形 愛する、愛情のこもった

□ **lower** 動 下げる、低くする

□ **loyal** 形 忠実な、誠実な

□ **loyalty** 图 忠義、忠誠

□ **lying** 動 lie（うそをつく・横たわる）の現在分詞

M

□ **Mac** 图 マック《マクドナルドの愛称》

□ **MacDonald, Inspector** マクドナルド警部補

□ **madam** 图 《ていねいな呼びかけ》奥様、お嬢様

□ **madden** 動 逆上させる、発狂させる

□ **main** 形 主な、主要な

□ **make** 國 make of 〜を理解する、解釈する、判断する make 〜 of ...…を〜と思う［理解する・受け取る・判断する］make one's mark 有名になる、名を成す［上げる］、頭角を現す make one's way into〔部屋など〕に入る make one's way to 〜に向かって進む make someone leave 退校［職］させる make too much of 〜を大げさに扱い過ぎる

□ **man** 間 うわ、やれやれ

□ **manager** 图 経営者、支配人、支店長、部長

□ **Manders** 图 マンダーズ《人名》

□ **manner** 图 ①方法、やり方 ②態度、様子 ③《-s》行儀、作法、生活様式

□ **manor** 图 ①荘園 ②警察の管轄区

□ **manor house** 領主の館

□ **many** 國 so many 非常に多くの

□ **mark** 图 ①印、記号、跡 ②点数 ③特色 動 ①印［記号］をつける ②採点する ③目立たせる make one's mark 有名になる、名を成す［上げる］、頭角を現す

□ **marriage** 图 ①結婚（生活・式）②結合、融合、（吸収）合併

□ **married** 動 marry（結婚する）の過去、過去分詞 形 結婚した、既婚の

□ **marry** 動 結婚する

□ **Marvin, Captain** マーヴィン警部

□ **Mason, White** ホワイト・メーソン《人名》

□ **master** 图 主人、雇い主、師、名匠

□ **matter** 图 a matter of 〜の問題 Supposing that a matter were to be brought secretly to his knowledge. あることが密かに彼の知るところとなったとしよう。

□ **May I 〜?** 〜してもいいですか。

□ **McGinty, Jack** ジャック・マギンティ《人名》

□ **McMurdo, Jack** ジャック・マクマードー《人名》

□ **McSomebody** 图 マックなんとかという人

□ **mean to** 〜するつもりである

□ **meaning** 图 ①意味、趣旨 ②重要性

□ **mean-looking** 形 意地の悪そうな、たちの悪そうな

□ **meeting** 图 ①集まり、ミーティング、面会 ②競技会

□ **membership** 图 会員、会員資格

□ **mention** 動 （〜について）述べる、言及する

□ **message** 國 coded message 暗号（化された）メッセージ、暗号文

□ **method** 图 ①方法、手段 ②秩序、体系

□ **middle-sized** 形 中背の

☐ **midnight** 名 夜の12時, 真夜中, 暗黒

☐ **might** 助《mayの過去》①～かもしれない ②～してもよい, ～できる

☐ **mighty** 形 強力な, 権勢のある

☐ **Mike Scanlan** マイク・スキャンラン《人名》

☐ **mile** 名 ①マイル《長さの単位。1,609m》②《-s》かなりの距離

☐ **Miller Hill** ミラー・ヒル《地名》

☐ **mind** 名 ①心, 精神, 考え ②知性 動 ①気にする, いやがる ②気をつける, 用心する

☐ **mine** 代 a friend of mine 友人の1人

☐ **miner** 名 炭鉱労働者, 坑夫

☐ **missing** 形 欠けている, 行方不明の

☐ **mister** 名《男性に対して》～さん, ～氏

☐ **mix** 動 ①混ざる, 混ぜる ②(～を)一緒にする

☐ **moat** 名 堀

☐ **moated** 形 堀のある

☐ **moment** 名 ①瞬間, ちょっとの間 ②(特定の)時, 時期 at the moment 今は for a moment 少しの間 for the moment 差し当たり, 当座は in a moment ただちに

☐ **more** 熟 more than ～以上 no more もう～ない once more もう一度

☐ **Moriarty, Professor** モリアーティ教授《人名》

☐ **Morris** 名 モリス《人名》

☐ **most** 熟 at the most せいぜい, 多くて

☐ **mostly** 副 主として, 多くは, ほとんど

☐ **motionless** 形 動きのない, 静止の

☐ **move in** 引っ越す

☐ **move to** ～に引っ越す

☐ **Mrs. Allen** アレン夫人

☐ **Mrs. Douglas** ダグラス夫人

☐ **much** 熟 make too much of ～を大げさに扱い過ぎる too much 過度の too much of あまりに～過ぎる

☐ **muddy** 形 泥だらけの, ぬかるみの

☐ **murder** 名 人殺し, 殺害, 殺人事件 動 殺す

☐ **murderer** 名 殺人犯

☐ **murmur** 名 つぶやき, かすかな音

☐ **mustache** 名《-s》口ひげ

☐ **my boy** (親しい)友達《呼びかけ》

☐ **mysterious** 形 神秘的な, 謎めいた

☐ **mysteriously** 副 神秘的に, 不思議に

☐ **mystery** 名 ①神秘, 不可思議 ②推理小説, ミステリー

N

☐ **Neal Outfitter** ニール洋服店《店名》

☐ **nearby** 形 近くの, 間近の 副 近くで, 間近で

☐ **nearly** 副 ①近くに, 親しく ②ほとんど, あやうく

☐ **necessary** 形 必要な, 必然の

☐ **neck** 熟 close one's hands around the other's neck 相手の首に手を回す

☐ **neither** 副《否定文に続いて》～も…しない

☐ **nervous** 形 ①神経の ②神経質な, おどおどした be nervous of〔～を〕少々怖がって

☐ **nervously** 副 神経質に, いらいらして

☐ **New York** ニューヨーク《米国の都市；州》

□ **newcomer** 图新しく来た人, 初心者

□ **news** 图報道, ニュース, 便り, 知らせ

□ **newspaper** 图新聞(紙)

□ **night before** 《the – 》前の晩

□ **nightfall** 图夕暮れ

□ **no** 熟come to no harm 危害を受けない, ひどい目に遭わない have no idea わからない no doubt きっと, たぶん no less やはり, 同様に no longer もはや～でない[～しない] no more もう～ない no one 誰も[一人も]～ない no use 役に立たない, 用をなさない of no use 《be ～》全く役に立たない, 用をなさない

□ **noise** 图騒音, 騒ぎ, 物音

□ **noisy** 形①騒々しい, やかましい ②けばけばしい

□ **nom-de-plume** 图筆名, ペンネーム

□ **none** 代(～の)何も[誰も・少しも]…ない

□ **nor** 接～もまたない

□ **not** 熟not ～ any longer もはや～でない[～しない] not at all 少しも～でない not ～ but ... ～ではなくて… not feel like doing ～する気になれない not likely ありそうもない, 可能性が低い not quite まったく～だというわけではない

□ **note** 图①メモ, 覚え書き ②注釈 ③注意, 注目 ④手形

□ **notebook** 图ノート, 手帳

□ **nothing** 熟all for nothing いたずらに, 無駄に can do nothing どうしようもない for nothing ただで, 無料で, むだに know nothing of ～のことを知らない

□ **notice** 動①気づく, 認める ②通告する

□ **now** 熟for now 今のところ, ひとまず from now 今から, これから now that 今や～だから, ～からには

right now 今すぐに, たった今 up to now 今まで

□ **nugget** 图(貴金属の)かたまり, 貴重なもの

□ **number** 熟a number of いくつかの～, 多くの～ the right number of 適度な枚数の

O

□ **object** 图①物, 事物 ②目的物, 対象

□ **observe** 動①観察[観測]する, 監視[注視]する ②気づく ③守る, 遵守する

□ **occupy** 動①占領する, 保有する ②居住する ③占める ④(職に)つく, 従事する

□ **occur** 動(事が)起こる, 生じる, (考えなどが)浮かぶ

□ **odd** 形①奇妙な ②奇数の ③(一対のうちの)片方の

□ **of no use** 《be ～》全く役に立たない, 用をなさない

□ **of one's own** 自分自身の

□ **Of that** それについて

□ **of which** ～の中で

□ **off** 熟get off (～から)降りる off the road 道路から離れたところに run off 走り去る, 逃げ去る set off 出発する, 発射する start off 出発する take off (衣服を)脱ぐ, 取り去る, ～を取り除く, 離陸する, 出発する

□ **offer** 動申し出る, 申し込む, 提供する

□ **office** 图会社, 事務所, 営業所, オフィス

□ **officer** 图役人, 公務員, 警察官 police officer 警察官

□ **oil** 图①油, 石油 ②油絵の具, 油絵

□ **old-world** 形旧世界の

□ **on** 熟on earth ①いったい ②地球

上で, この世で **on guard against** 〜に備えて警戒している **on one's feet** 立っている状態で **on one's guard** 〔危険・敵などに対して〕警戒〔用心・注意〕する **on one's way** 途中で **on one's way to** 〜に行く途中で **on the spot** すぐその場で, 直ちに, 即座に

☐ **once** 熟 **at once** すぐに, 同時に **once more** もう一度

☐ **one** 熟 **no one** 誰も〔一人も〕〜ない **one of** 〜の1つ〔人〕 **one side** 片側

☐ **oneself** 熟 **by oneself** 一人で, 自分だけで, 独力で **for oneself** 独力で, 自分のために

☐ **operator** 名オペレーター, 交換手, 操作する人

☐ **opposite** 形反対の, 向こう側の

☐ **or so** 〜かそこらで

☐ **order** 熟 **law and order** 治安, 法と秩序

☐ **Order of Freemen** 自由民団

☐ **organization** 名①組織(化), 編成, 団体, 機関 ②有機体, 生物

☐ **out** 熟 **be out** 消えている **be scared out of** 〜で腰を抜かす, 〜で気が動転する **call out** 叫ぶ, 呼び出す, 声を掛ける **come out** 出てくる, 出掛ける, 姿を現す, 発行される **come out of** 〜から出てくる, 〜をうまく乗り越える **cry out** 叫ぶ **draw out** 引き抜く **get out** ①外に出る, 出て行く, 逃げ出す ②取り出す, 抜き出す **go out** 外出する, 外へ出る, 消灯する **hold out** ①差し出す, (腕を)伸ばす ②持ちこたえる, 粘る, 耐える **look out** ①外を見る ②気をつける, 注意する **look out of** (窓などから)外を見る **out of** ①〜から外へ, 〜から抜け出して ②〜から作り出して, 〜を材料として ③〜の範囲外に, 〜から離れて ④(ある数)の中から **pour one's troubles out** 悩みを打ち明ける **pull out** 引き抜く, 引き出す, 取り出す **push out** 突き出す

read out 声を出して読む, 読み上げる **rush out** 急いで〔性急に〕出て行く **sell out** 売り切る, 裏切る **take out** 取り出す, 取り外す, 連れ出す, 持って帰る **throw out** 放り出す

☐ **outer** 形外の, 外側の

☐ **outfitter** 名洋服店

☐ **outline** 名①外形, 輪郭 ②概略

☐ **outsider** 名よそ者, 部外者, 門外漢

☐ **over** 熟 **be over** 終わる **go over to** 〜の前に〔へ〕行く, 〜に出向いて行く **hang over** 〔危険が〕差し迫る, 〜を脅かす **lean over** 〜にかがみ込む **over and over** 何度も繰り返して **take over** 引き受ける **watch over** 見守る, 見張る

☐ **overboard** 副船外へ

☐ **overcoat** 名オーバー, 外套

☐ **owe** 動①(〜を)負う, (〜を人の)お陰とする ②(金を)借りている, (人に対して〜の)義務がある

☐ **own** 熟 **of one's own** 自分自身の

☐ **owner** 名持ち主, オーナー

P

☐ **page** 名小姓, ボーイ

☐ **page system** ページ方式

☐ **painful** 形①痛い, 苦しい, 痛ましい ②骨の折れる, 困難な

☐ **painter** 名画家, ペンキ屋

☐ **painting** 名①絵(をかくこと), 絵画, 油絵 ②ペンキ塗装

☐ **pair** 名(2つから成る)一対, 一組, ペア

☐ **pale** 形①(顔色・人が)青ざめた, 青白い ②(色が)薄い, (光が)薄暗い

☐ **pantry** 名食品貯蔵室

☐ **paper** 熟 **faked paper** 偽札

☐ **parlor** 名①パーラー, 店 ②客間 ③休憩室

A
B
C
D
E
F
G
H
I
J
K
L
M
N
O
P
Q
R
S
T
U
V
W
X
Y
Z

- **particular** 形 ①特別の ②詳細な
- **particularly** 副 特に, とりわけ
- **partner** 名 配偶者, 仲間, 同僚
- **passage** 名 ①通過, 通行, 通路 ②一節, 経過
- **passenger** 名 乗客, 旅客
- **past** 形 過去の, この前の 名 過去(の出来事) 副《時間・場所》~を過ぎて, ~を越して
- **patch** 継ぎはぎ, 継ぎ, 傷当て **Hobson's Patch** ホブソンズ・パッチ《地名》
- **path** 名 ①(踏まれてできた)小道, 歩道 ②進路, 通路
- **pause** 名 ①(活動の)中止, 休止 ②区切り
- **pay** 動 ①支払う, 払う, 報いる, 償う ②割に合う, ペイする
- **peace** 熟 **in peace** 平和のうちに, 安心して
- **peaceful** 形 平和な, 穏やかな
- **Pennsylvania Small Arms Company** ペンシルベニア小火器会社
- **perhaps** 副 たぶん, ことによると
- **Philadelphia** 名 フィラデルフィア《地名》
- **physically** 副 ①自然法則上, 物理的に ②肉体的に, 身体的に
- **pick up** 拾い上げる
- **Pinkerton's** 名 ピンカートン探偵社
- **Pinto, Jonas** ジョナス・ピント《人名》
- **pipe** 名 管, 筒, パイプ
- **place** 熟 **take place**〔事前に計画されたことが〕行われる,〔災害・事故などが偶然に〕起こる
- **plain** 形 ①明白な, はっきりした ②簡素な ③平らな ④不細工な, 平凡な 名 高原, 草原
- **plan to do** ~するつもりである

- **plaster** 名 ①しっくい, 壁土, 石膏 ②ばんそうこう, 膏薬
- **please** 熟 **if you please** よろしければ
- **pleased** 形 喜んだ, 気に入った
- **pleasing** 形 心地のよい, 楽しい
- **pleasure** 名 喜び, 楽しみ, 満足, 娯楽
- **police officer** 警察官
- **policeman** 名 警察官
- **policemen** 名 policeman(警察官)の複数
- **popularity** 名 人気, 流行
- **Porlock, Fred** フレッド・ポーロック《人名》
- **possible** 形 ①可能な ②ありうる, 起こりうる
- **possibly** 副 ①あるいは, たぶん ②《否定文, 疑問文で》どうしても, できる限り, とても, なんとか
- **pound** 名 ①ポンド《英国の通貨単位》②ポンド《重量の単位。453.6g》
- **pour** 動 ①注ぐ, 浴びせる ②流れ出る, 流れ込む ③ざあざあ降る **pour one's troubles out** 悩みを打ち明ける
- **powerful** 形 力強い, 実力のある, 影響力のある
- **powerless** 形 力のない, 頼りない, 弱い
- **preparation** 名 ①準備, したく ②心構え
- **prepare for** ~の準備をする
- **pretend** 動 ①ふりをする, 装う ②あえて~しようとする
- **previous** 形 前の, 先の
- **price** 名 ①値段, 代価 ②《-s》物価, 相場
- **pride** 名 誇り, 自慢, 自尊心
- **prison** 名 ①刑務所, 監獄 ②監禁
- **private** 形 ①私的な, 個人の ②民間の, 私立の ③内密の, 人里離れた

□ **probably** 副 たぶん, あるいは

□ **proceed** 動 進む, 進展する, 続ける

□ **professor** 名 教授, 師匠

□ **Professor Moriarty** モリアーティ教授《人名》

□ **progress** 名 ①進歩, 前進 ②成り行き, 経過

□ **propose** 動 ①申し込む, 提案する ②結婚を申し込む

□ **protection** 名 保護, 保護するもの [人]

□ **protest** 動 ①主張[断言]する ②抗議する, 反対する

□ **prove** 動 ①証明する ②(〜てあることが) わかる, (〜と) なる

□ **public** 形 公の, 公開の

□ **pull out** 引き抜く, 引き出す, 取り出す

□ **pull up** 引っ張り上げる

□ **punish** 動 罰する, ひどい目にあわせる

□ **punishment** 名 ①罰, 処罰 ②罰を受けること

□ **push back** 押し返す, 押しのける

□ **push one's way through the crowd** 人混みの中を押し分けて進む

□ **push out** 突き出す

□ **push through** (人ごみなどを) かき分ける

□ **put** 熟 put back (もとの場所に) 戻す, 返す put down 下に置く, 下ろす put in 〜の中に入れる put ... into ... 〜を…の状態にする, 〜を…に突っ込む put on ①〜を身につける, 着る ②〜を…の上に置く put the fear of death into (人) をひどく怖がらせる, (人) をびびらせる

□ **puzzled** 形 当惑した, 困惑した

Q

□ **quarrel** 動 けんかする, 口論する

□ **quarter** 名 ①4分の1, 25セント, 15分, 3カ月 ②方面, 地域 ③部署 quarter to 〜時15分前

□ **quickly** 副 敏速に, 急いで

□ **quietly** 副 ①静かに ②平穏に, 控えめに

□ **quiet-natured** 形 静かな, 穏やかな, 内気な

□ **quit** 動 やめる, 辞職する, 中止する

□ **quite** 熟 not quite まったく〜だというわけではない

R

□ **railroad** 名 鉄道, 路線

□ **raise** 動 ①上げる, 高める ②起こす ③〜を育てる ④(資金を) 調達する

□ **rang** 動 ring (鳴る) の過去

□ **range** 名 列, 連なり, 範囲

□ **rather** 副 ①むしろ, かえって ②かなり, いくぶん, やや ③それどころか逆に would rather 〜する方がよい

□ **read out** 声を出して読む, 読み上げる

□ **reader** 名 ①読者 ②読本, リーダー

□ **ready to** 《be 〜》すぐに[いつでも] 〜できる, 〜する構えで ready to go すっかり準備が整った

□ **recently** 副 近ごろ, 最近

□ **recognizable** 動 見覚えがある, 認識できる

□ **recognize** 動 認める, 認識[承認]する

□ **recommend** 動 ①推薦する ②勧告する, 忠告する

□ **recover** 動 ①取り戻す, ばん回す

る ②回復する

□ **refuse** 動拒絶する，断る

□ **regularly** 副整然と，規則的に

□ **Reilly** 名ライリー《人名》

□ **relax** 動①くつろがせる ②ゆるめる，緩和する

□ **remain** 動①残っている，残る ②（～の）ままである［いる］

□ **remaining** 形残った，残りの

□ **remark** 動①注目する ②述べる，批評する

□ **remarkable** 形①異常な，例外的な ②注目に値する，すばらしい

□ **remind** 動思い出させる，気づかせる

□ **remove** 動①取り去る，除去する ②（衣類を）脱ぐ

□ **renew** 動新しくする，更新する，回復する，再開する

□ **repeat** 動繰り返す

□ **replace** 動①取り替える，差し替える ②元に戻す

□ **reply** 名答え，返事，応答

□ **reporter** 名レポーター，報告者，記者

□ **represent** 動①表現する ②意味する ③代表する

□ **respect** 名①尊敬，尊重 ②注意，考慮 動尊敬［尊重］する

□ **respectable** 形①尊敬すべき，立派な ②（量など）相当な

□ **restful** 形落ち着かない，不安な

□ **result** 名結果，成り行き，成績 動（結果として）起こる，生じる，結局～になる

□ **revenge** 名復讐

□ **right** 熟 all right 大丈夫で，よろしい，申し分ない，わかった，承知した **right now** 今すぐに，たった今 **the right number of** 適度な枚数の

□ **ring** 名①輪，円形，指輪 ②競技場，リング 動①輪で取り囲む ②鳴る，

鳴らす ③電話をかける

□ **ringing** 名（鐘がなる）音

□ **road** 熟 off the road 道路から離れたところに

□ **roar** 名①ほえ声，怒号 ②大笑い

□ **rob** 動奪う，金品を盗む，襲う

□ **roll** 動①転がる，転がす ②（波などが）うねる，横揺れする ③（時が）たつ **roll up** 巻き上げる

□ **room** 熟 dining room 食堂 **take a room** （宿で）部屋を取る **waiting room** 待合室

□ **rope** 名綱，なわ，ロープ

□ **rough** 形①（手触りが）粗い ②荒々しい，未加工の

□ **round** 熟 go round ～の周りを進む，歩き回る，回って行く

□ **rude** 形粗野な，無作法な，失礼な

□ **rule of fear** 恐怖による支配

□ **rule ~ with a heavy hand** ～を厳しく統治［支配］する

□ **run across** 走って渡る

□ **run off** 走り去る，逃げ去る

□ **rush** 動突進する，せき立てる **rush down** 猛然と～に駆け寄る **rush in** ～に突入する，～に駆けつける **rush out** 急いで［性急に］出て行く

S

□ **sadly** 副悲しそうに，不幸にも

□ **safety** 名安全，無事，確実

□ **sake** 名（～の）ため，利益，目的 **for god's sake** 一生のお願いだから，どうかお願いだから

□ **salary** 名給料

□ **saloon** 名①大広間，談話室 ②セダン型の自動車，サルーン ③酒場

□ **Scanlan, Mike** マイク・スキャンラン《人名》

□ **scared** 形おびえた，びっくりした **be scared out of** ～で腰を抜かす，～で気が動転する

□ **scientific** 形科学の，科学的な

□ **Scotland Yard** ロンドン警視庁の通称，愛称

□ **Scotsman** 名スコットランド人

□ **Scowrers** 名スカウラーズ《秘密結社の名》

□ **scream** 動叫ぶ，金切り声を出す

□ **search** 動捜し求める，調べる

□ **secrecy** 名秘密であること

□ **secret** 形①秘密の，隠れた ②神秘の，不思議な 名秘密，神秘 **secret code** 暗号

□ **secretly** 副秘密に，内緒で

□ **see** 熟 **see ～ as ...** ～を…と考える **see if** ～かどうかを確かめる，～かどうかを見る **you see** あのね，いいですわ

□ **seem** 動（～に）見える，（～のように）思われる **seem to be** ～であるように思われる

□ **self-defense** 名自衛，自己防衛，正当防衛

□ **sell out** 売り切る，裏切る

□ **sense** 名①感覚，感じ ②《-s》意識，正気，本性 ③常識，分別，センス ④意味

□ **separate** 動①分ける，分かれる，隔てる ②別れる，別れさせる

□ **sergeant** 名①軍曹，巡査部長 ②上級法廷弁護士

□ **Sergeant Wilson** ウィルソン巡査部長

□ **serious** 形①まじめな，真剣な ②重大な，深刻な，（病気などが）重い

□ **seriously** 副①真剣に，まじめに ②重大に

□ **servant** 名①召使，使用人，しもべ ②公務員，（公共事業の）従業員

□ **service** 名①勤務，業務 ②公益事業 ③点検，修理 ④奉仕，貢献

□ **set off** 出発する，発射する

□ **settle** 動①安定する［させる］，落ち着く，落ち着かせる ②《– in ～》～に移り住む，定住する **settle down** 落ち着く，興奮がおさまる

□ **seventeenth** 名17，17人［個］形17の，17人［個］の

□ **shadow** 名①影，暗がり ②亡霊

□ **Shafter, Ettie** エティー・シャフター《人名》

□ **Shafter, Jacob** ジェイコブ・シャフター《人名》

□ **shake** 動①振る，揺れる，揺さぶる，震える ②動揺させる **shake hands** 握手をする

□ **shaken** 動shake（振る）の過去分詞

□ **shape** 動形づくる，具体化する

□ **sharp** 形①鋭い，とがった ②刺すような，きつい ③鋭敏な ④急な

□ **shave** 動（ひげ・顔を）そる，削る

□ **Sheridan Street** シェリダン通り

□ **Sherlock Holmes** シャーロック・ホームズ《観察力と推理力に優れた探偵》

□ **shine** 動①光る，輝く ②光らせる，磨く

□ **shocked** 形～にショックを受けて，憤慨して

□ **shone** 動shine（光る）の過去，過去分詞

□ **shook** 動shake（振る）の過去

□ **shooting** 名射殺

□ **shotgun** 名散弾銃

□ **shoulder** 名肩

□ **shut** 動①閉まる，閉める，閉じる ②たたむ ③閉じ込める ④shutの過去，過去分詞

□ **side** 名側，横，そば，斜面 形①側面の，横の ②副次的な **far side** 向こ

う側, 反対側 one side 片側

□ **silence** 图沈黙, 無言, 静寂 in silence 黙って, 沈黙のうちに

□ **sill** 图〔窓・戸などの〕敷居 window sill 窓台

□ **simply** 副①簡単に ②単に, ただ ③まったく, 完全に

□ **single** 形①たった1つの ②1人用の, それぞれの ③独身の ④片道の

□ **sit still** じっとしている, じっと座っている

□ **situation** 图①場所, 位置 ②状況, 境遇, 立場

□ **slam** 動ばたんと閉まる, 急に閉じる 图ばたん(という音)

□ **slamming** 图バタンと閉めること

□ **sleeve** 图袖, たもと, スリーブ

□ **slip** 動滑る, 滑らせる, 滑って転ぶ

□ **slipper** 图①《通例-s》部屋ばき, スリッパ ②(車の)歯止め carpet slippers 屋内用スリッパ

□ **slowly** 副遅く, ゆっくり

□ **smile at** ～に微笑みかける

□ **smoke** 動喫煙する, 煙を出す

□ **so** 熟and so そこで, それだから, それで or so ～かそこらで so far 今までのところ, これまでは so long as ～する限りは so many 非常に多くの so that ～するために, それで, ～できるように so ～ that ... 非常に～なので…

□ **society** 图社会, 世間

□ **sock** 图《-s》ソックス, 靴下

□ **softly** 副柔らかに, 優しく, そっと

□ **solution** 图①分解, 溶解 ②解決, 解明, 回答

□ **solve** 動解く, 解決する

□ **some** 熟at some time ある時点[時期]に for some time しばらくの間 in some way 何とかして, 何らかの方法で

□ **someone** 代ある人, 誰か

□ **Somerton, Dr.** ソーマートン医師《人名》

□ **something** 代①ある物, 何か ②いくぶん, 多少

□ **sometimes** 副時々, 時たま

□ **somewhat** 副いくらか, やや, 多少

□ **somewhere** 副①どこかへ[に] ②いつか, およそ

□ **sore** 形①痛い, 傷のある ②悲惨な, ひどい

□ **sort** 图種類, 品質 a sort of ～のようなもの, 一種の～ what sort of どういう

□ **soul** 图①魂 ②精神, 心

□ **speak about** ～について話す

□ **speak of** ～を口にする

□ **speak to** ～と話す

□ **speedily** 副早く, 急いで

□ **spot** 图①地点, 場所, 立場 ②斑点, しみ on the spot すぐその場で, 直ちに, 即座に

□ **sprang** 動spring (跳ねる)の過去

□ **square** 形①正方形の, 四角な, 直角な, 角ばった ②平方の

□ **St. Helena** セントヘレナ《島名》

□ **stain** 動〔～に〕染みを付ける, 〔～を〕汚す

□ **stair** 图①(階段の)1段 ②《-s》階段, はしご

□ **staircase** 图階段

□ **stand for** ～を意味する, ～を支持する, ～を我慢する, ～をこらえる

□ **Stanger, James** ジェームズ・ステンジャー《人名》

□ **stare** 動じっと[じろじろ]見る 图じっと見ること, 凝視

□ **start doing** ～し始める

□ **start off** 出発する

□ **start to do** ～し始める

- [ ] **started** 熟 get started 始める
- [ ] **state** 名 ①あり様, 状態 ②国家, (アメリカなどの) 州 ③階層, 地位
- [ ] **stay in** 家にいる, (場所)に泊まる, 滞在する
- [ ] **Steve Wilson** スティーヴ・ウィルソン《人名》
- [ ] **stick** 名 棒, 杖
- [ ] **still** 熟 sit still じっとしている, じっと座っている
- [ ] **stir** 動 動かす, かき回す **stir up** かき混ぜる, かき回す
- [ ] **stolen** 動 steal (盗む) の過去分詞
- [ ] **stop doing** ～するのをやめる
- [ ] **storm** 名 ①嵐, 暴風雨 ②強襲
- [ ] **stranger** 名 ①見知らぬ人, 他人 ②不案内[不慣れ]な人
- [ ] **strict** 形 厳しい, 厳密な
- [ ] **strike down** (人)を打ち倒す, (人)を殺す
- [ ] **strongly** 副 強く, 頑丈に, 猛烈に, 熱心に
- [ ] **struck** 動 strike (打つ) の過去, 過去分詞
- [ ] **struggle** 名 もがき, 奮闘
- [ ] **stuff** 名 ①材料, 原料 ②もの, 持ち物
- [ ] **succeed** 動 ①成功する ②(～の) 跡を継ぐ
- [ ] **success** 名 成功, 幸運, 上首尾
- [ ] **such** 熟 in such a way そのような方法で **such a** そのような **such ～ as ...** …のような～
- [ ] **sudden** 形 突然の, 急な
- [ ] **suggest** 動 ①提案する ②示唆する
- [ ] **suggestion** 名 ①提案, 忠告 ②気配, 暗示
- [ ] **suit** 名 ①スーツ, 背広 ②訴訟 ③ひとそろい, 一組
- [ ] **suited** 形 適した

- [ ] **suppose** 動 ①仮定する, 推測する ②《be -d to ～》～することになっている, ～するものである **Supposing that a matter were to be brought secretly to his knowledge.** あることが密かに彼の知るところとなったとしよう。
- [ ] **sure enough** 思ったとおり, 案の定
- [ ] **surely** 副 確かに, きっと
- [ ] **surprise** 熟 be taken by surprise 意を突かれる, やみ打ちを食う to one's surprise ～が驚いたことに
- [ ] **surprised** 形 驚いた
- [ ] **surprising** 形 驚くべき, 意外な
- [ ] **surround** 動 囲む, 包囲する
- [ ] **Sussex** 名 サセックス《地名》
- [ ] **sweep from** ～からさっと通り過ぎる
- [ ] **swept** 動 sweep (掃く) の過去, 過去分詞
- [ ] **swing** 形 揺れ動く **swinging door** スイングドア
- [ ] **sworn** 動 swear (誓う) の過去分詞
- [ ] **swung** 動 swing (回転する) の過去, 過去分詞
- [ ] **system** 熟 page system ページ方式

T

- [ ] **take** 熟 take a good look at ～ をよく見る **take a room** (宿で) 部屋を取る **take a walk** 散歩をする **take from** ～から引く, 選ぶ **take off** (衣服を) 脱ぐ, 取り去る, ～を取り除く, 離陸する, 出発する **take out** 取り出す, 取り外す, 連れ出す, 持って帰る **take over** 引き受ける **take place** [事前に計画されたことが] 行われる, [災害・事故などが偶然に] 起こる **take someone away**

（人）を連れ出す **take someone on trust** （人）を信じる

□ **taken** 熟 **be taken by surprise** 意を突かれる, やみ打ちを食う

□ **talk** 熟 **have a talk** 話をする **talk of** ～のことを話す

□ **Ted Baldwin** テッド・ボールドウィン《人名》

□ **Teddy Baldwin** テディ・ボールドウィン《人名》

□ **telegram** 名 電報

□ **tell ～ to ...** ～に…するように言う

□ **terribly** 副 ひどく

□ **terror** 名 ①恐怖 ②恐ろしい人[物]

□ **than** 熟 **more than** ～以上

□ **Thank God.** ありがたい

□ **that** 熟 **at that time** その時 **now that** 今や～だから, ～からには **Of that** それについて **so that** ～するために, それで, ～できるように **so ～ that ...** 非常に～なので…

□ **therefore** 副 したがって, それゆえ, その結果

□ **thick** 形 厚い, 密集した, 濃厚な

□ **thief** 名 泥棒, 強盗

□ **thin** 形 薄い, 細い, やせた, まばらな

□ **think of** ～のことを考える, ～を思いつく, 考え出す

□ **thirtieth** 形 ①《the -》30番目の ②30分の1の 名 ①《the -》30番目 ②30分の1

□ **this** 熟 **at this** これを見て, そこで（すぐに）**this way** このように

□ **those who** ～する人々

□ **though** 接 ①～にもかかわらず, ～だが ②たとえ～でも 副 しかし **even though** ～であるけれども, ～にもかかわらず

□ **thoughtfully** 副 考え[思いやり]深く

□ **thousands of** 何千という

□ **threateningly** 副 脅迫的に, 脅して

□ **throat** 名 のど, 気管

□ **through** 熟 **break through ～** を打ち破る **come through** 通り抜ける, 成功する, 期待に沿う **push one's way through the crowd** 人混みの中を押し分けて進む **push through**（人ごみなどを）かき分ける

□ **throw down** 投げ出す, 放棄する

□ **throw out** 放り出す

□ **thrown** 動 throw（投げる）の過去分詞

□ **tiger** 名 ①トラ（虎）②あばれ者

□ **tighten** 動 ①ぴんと張る, 堅く締める ②余裕がなくなる ③厳しくなる

□ **till** 接 ～（する）まで

□ **time** 熟 **at some time** ある時点[時期]に **at that time** その時 **at the time** そのころ, 当時は **back in time** 過去に戻る, 時をさかのぼる **for a time** しばらく, 一時の間 **for some time** しばらくの間 **just in time** いよいよというときに, すんでのところで, やっと間に合って **the last time** この前～したとき

□ **tired** 形 ①疲れた, くたびれた ②あきた, うんざりした **be tired of ～** に飽きた[うんざりして]いる

□ **to** 熟 **to one's feet** 両足で立っている状態に **to one's surprise** ～が驚いたことに **too ～ to ...** …するには～すぎる

□ **toe** 名 足指, つま先

□ **tone** 名 音, 音色, 調子

□ **too** 熟 **make too much of ～** を大げさに扱い過ぎる **too much** 過度の **too much of** あまりに～過ぎる **too ～ to ...** …するには～すぎる

□ **touch** 熟 **in touch** 連絡を取って **touch up** 少し変える, 修正する

□ **trace** 動 たどる, さかのぼって調べ

る

□ **tragedy** 名悲劇, 惨劇

□ **trail** 名(通った)跡

□ **traitor** 名反逆者, 裏切り者

□ **trap** 名わな, 策略 動わなを仕掛ける, わなで捕らえる

□ **trapping** 名わな

□ **traveler** 名旅行者

□ **trial** 名①試み, 試験 ②苦難 ③裁判

□ **triangle** 名①三角形 ②トライアングル《楽器》

□ **trouble** 熟 get into trouble 面倒を起こす, 困った事になる, トラブルに巻き込まれる In trouble 面倒な状況で, 困って pour one's troubles out 悩みを打ち明ける

□ **trust** 動信用[信頼]する, 委託する 名信用, 信頼, 委託 take someone on trust (人)を信じる

□ **truth** 名①真理, 事実, 本当 ②誠実, 忠実さ

□ **truthful** 形正直な, 真実の

□ **Tunbridge Wells** タンブリッジ・ウェルズ《地名》

□ **turn to** ～の方を向く, ～に頼る, ～に変わる

□ **turn up** 〔裾・縁・袖口を〕上へ折り返す

□ **turning** 名回転, 曲がり角

□ **two** 熟 a ～ or two 1～か2～, 2, 3の

U

□ **U.S.A.** 略米国

□ **ugly** 形①醜い, ぶかっこうな ②いやな, 不快な, 険悪な

□ **uncomfortable** 形心地よくない

□ **underclothes** 名下着, 肌着

□ **undid** 動 undo (ほどく) の過去

□ **undiscovered** 形発見されていない

□ **undo** 動元へ戻す, 取り消す, ほどく

□ **unexpected** 形思いがけない, 予期しない

□ **unfold** 動①(折りたたんだものを)広げる, 開く ②(計画などを)知らせる, 明らかになる

□ **union** 名①結合, 合併, 融合 ②連合国家

□ **Union House** ユニオン・ハウス

□ **United States** 《the –》アメリカ合衆国《国名》

□ **unmarried** 形未婚の, 独身の

□ **untrusting** 形明らかに不信で

□ **unusual** 形普通でない, 珍しい, 見[聞き]慣れない

□ **up** 熟 blow up 破裂する[させる] break up ばらばらになる, 解散させる bring up ①育てる, 連れて行く ②(問題を)持ち出す come up 近づいてくる, 階上に行く, 浮上する, 水面上に上ってくる, 発生する, 芽を出す come up with ～に行きつく give up あきらめる, やめる, 引き渡す halfway up 半ばまで上った所に keep up 続ける, 続く, 維持する, (遅れないで) ついていく, 上げたままにしておく look up 見上げる, 調べる pick up 拾い上げる pull up 引っ張り上げる roll up 巻き上げる stir up かき混ぜる, かき回す touch up 少し変える, 修正する turn up 〔裾・縁・袖口を〕上へ折り返す up to ～まで, ～に至るまで, ～に匹敵して up to now 今まで walk up 歩み寄る, 歩いて上る walk up to ～に歩み寄る

□ **upon** 前①《場所・接触》～(の上)に ②《日・時》～に ③《関係・従事》～に関して, ～について, ～して

□ **upper** 形上の, 上位の, 北方の

□ **upstairs** 副2階へ[に], 階上へ

A
B
C
D
E
F
G
H
I
J
K
L
M
N
O
P
Q
R
S
T
U
V
W
X
Y
Z

□ **urge** 動①せき立てる, 強力に推し進める, かりたてる ②《 – ... to 〜》…に〜するよう熱心に勧める

□ **urgent** 形緊急の, 差し迫った

□ **use** 熟in common use《 be 〜》一般的に使われて [用いられて] いる **no use** 役に立たない, 用をなさない **of no use**《 be 〜》全く役に立たない, 用をなさない

□ **used** 動①use (使う) の過去, 過去分詞 ②《 – to》よく〜したものだ, 以前は〜であった 形①慣れている, 《 get [become] – to》〜に慣れてくる ②使われた, 中古の

□ **usual** 形通常の, いつもの, 平常の, 普通の **as usual** いつものように, 相変わらず

V

□ **valley** 名谷, 谷間

□ **valuable** 形貴重な, 価値のある, 役に立つ

□ **Vermissa** 名ヴァーミッサ《地名》

□ **Vermissa Herald** ヴァーミッサ・ヘラルド《新聞 (社) の名》

□ **Vermissa Lodge** ヴァーミッサ支部

□ **Vermissa Valley** ヴァーミッサ谷

□ **very likely** たぶん

□ **very well** 結構, よろしい

□ **villager** 名村人, 田舎の人

□ **violently** 副激しく, 猛烈に, 暴力的に

□ **visitor** 名訪問客

□ **volume** 名①本, 巻, 冊 ②《-s》たくさん, 多量 ③量, 容積

□ **vote** 動投票する, 投票して決める

W

□ **wait for** 〜を待つ

□ **waiting** 名待機, 給仕すること

□ **waiting room** 待合室

□ **walk** 熟take a walk 散歩をする **walk across** 〜を歩いて渡る **walk around** 歩き回る, ぶらぶら歩く **walk up** 歩み寄る, 歩いて上る **walk up to** 〜に歩み寄る

□ **warn** 動警告する, 用心させる

□ **warning** 名警告, 警報

□ **watch over** 見守る, 見張る

□ **Watson** 名ワトソン《人名》

□ **wave** 名①波 ②(手などを) 振ること 動①揺れる, 揺らす, 波立つ ②(手などを振って) 合図する

□ **way** 熟all the way ずっと, はるばる, いろいろと **by the way** ところで, ついでに **come all the way from** はるばる〜からやって来る **go on one's way** 道を進む, 立ち去る **in some way** 何とかして, 何らかの方法で **in such a way** そのような方法で **make one's way into** 〔部屋など〕に入る **make one's way to** 〜に向かって進む **on one's way** 途中で **on one's way to** 〜に行く途中で **one's way to** (〜への) 途中で **push one's way through the crowd** 人混みの中を押し分けて進む **this way** このように **way of** 〜する方法 **way to** 〜する方法

□ **weakly** 副弱々しく

□ **weakness** 名①弱さ, もろさ ②欠点, 弱点

□ **wealthy** 形裕福な, 金持ちの

□ **weapon** 名武器, 兵器 **why this gun, of all weapons?** よりによって, なぜこの銃なのか?

□ **wedding** 名結婚式, 婚礼

□ **weigh 〜 down** 〔重さで〕垂れ下がらせる

□ **weight** 動①重みをつける ②重荷

□ **well** 熟 be well -ed よく［十分に］
～された **very well** 結構，よろしい
well done うまくやった

□ **well-educated** 形 教養のある

□ **well-known** 形 よく知られた，有
名な

□ **well-organized** 形 よく組織さ
れた，うまくまとまった

□ **Westville Arms** ウェストビル・
アームズ《宿泊先の名》

□ **westward** 名 西方

□ **wet** 形 ぬれた，湿った，雨の

□ **What about ～?** ～についてあ
なたはどう思いますか。～はどうです
か。

□ **what ... for** どんな目的で

□ **what if** もし～だったらどうなる
だろうか

□ **what sort of** どういう

□ **whatever** 代 ①《関係代名詞》～
するものは何でも ②どんなこと［も
の］が～とも

□ **whether** 接 ～かどうか，～かまた
は…，～であろうとなかろうと

□ **which** 熟 of which ～の中で

□ **while** 熟 for a while しばらくの間，
少しの間

□ **whisper** 動 ささやく，小声で話す

□ **White Mason** ホワイト・メーソ
ン《人名》

□ **who** 熟 those who ～する人々

□ **whole** 形 全体の，すべての，完全な，
満～，丸～

□ **whom** 代 ①誰を［に］②《関係代
名詞》～するところの人，そしてその
人を

□ **why this gun, of all weapons?**
よりによって，なぜこの銃なのか？

□ **wicked** 形 悪い，不道徳な

□ **wide** 形 幅の広い，広範囲の，幅が
～ある

□ **Will you ～?** ～してくれませんか。

□ **willing** 形 ①喜んで～する，～して
も構わない，いとわない ②自分から
進んで行う

□ **Wilson, Steve** スティーヴ・ウィ
ルソン《人名》

□ **win someone's heart**（人）の
ハートを射止める

□ **winding** 形 曲がりくねった

□ **window sill** 窓台

□ **winner** 名 勝利者，成功者

□ **wish** 熟 good wishes 好意，厚情

□ **with all** ～がありながら

□ **with fear** 怖がって

□ **within** 副 ①～の中［内］に，～の内
部に ②～以内で，～を越えないで

□ **without fail** 必ず，確実に

□ **witness** 名 ①証拠，証言 ②目撃
者

□ **wonder** 動 ①不思議に思う，（～
に）驚く ②（～かしらと）思う

□ **work** 熟 at work 働いて，仕事中で，
（機械が）稼働中で **work in** ～の分野
で働く，～に入り込む **work of** ～の
仕事

□ **workmen** 名 workman（労働者）
の複数

□ **world** 熟 in the world 世界で

□ **worried** 形 心配そうな，不安げな

□ **worse** 形 いっそう悪い，より劣っ
た，よりひどい

□ **worst** 形《the －》最も悪い，いちば
んひどい 名《the －》最悪の事態［人・
物］

□ **would like** ～がほしい

□ **would like to** ～したいと思う

□ **would rather** ～する方がよい

□ **Would you ～?** ～してください
ませんか。

□ **wounded** 形 傷ついた

□ **write down** 書き留める

A
B
C
D
E
F
G
H
I
J
K
L
M
N
O
P
Q
R
S
T
U
V
W
X
Y
Z

☐ **write to** 〜に手紙を書く

☐ **writing** 動write（書く）の現在分詞 名①書くこと，作文，著述 ②筆跡 ③書き物，書かれたもの，文書

☐ **wrong with** 《be −》（〜にとって）よくない，〜が故障している

Y

☐ **years** 熟for 〜 years 〜年間，〜年にわたって

☐ **yell** 動大声をあげる，わめく

☐ **yet** 熟and yet それなのに，それにもかかわらず

☐ **you know** ご存知のとおり，そうでしょう

☐ **you see** あのね，いいですか

☐ **yourselves** 代yourself（あなた自身）の複数

☐ **youthful** 形若々しい

A
B
C
D
E
F
G
H
I
J
K
L
M
N
O
P
Q
R
S
T
U
V
W
X
Y
Z

English Conversational Ability Test
国際英語会話能力検定

● E-CATとは…
英語が話せるようになるための
テストです。インターネット
ベースで、30分であなたの発
話力をチェックします。

● iTEP®とは…
世界各国の企業、政府機関、アメリカの大学
300校以上が、英語能力判定テストとして採用。
オンラインによる90分のテストで文法、リー
ディング、リスニング、ライティング、スピー
キングの5技能をスコア化。iTEP®は、留学、就
職、海外赴任などに必要な、世界に通用する英
語力を総合的に評価する画期的なテストです。

| www.ecatexam.com |
| www.itepexamjapan.com |

ラダーシリーズ

The Valley of Fear
シャーロック・ホームズ／恐怖の谷

2024 年 7 月 11 日　第 1 刷発行

原著者　　コナン・ドイル

発行者　　賀川　洋

発行所　　IBCパブリッシング株式会社
　　　　　〒162-0804 東京都新宿区中里町29番3号
　　　　　菱秀神楽坂ビル
　　　　　Tel. 03-3513-4511　Fax. 03-3513-4512
　　　　　www.ibcpub.co.jp

印刷　株式会社シナノパブリッシングプレス

装丁　伊藤 理恵　カバーイラスト　田口 智子

Printed in Japan
ISBN978-4-7946-0820-8